For
Anna and Erin
Sara, Jeannette, Reiner, Lucy and Rose
Christopher

Pilgrims all
— G. D. S.

To Donald Hall,
for whom work is the daily text of the life lived.
— B. M.

John Bunyan

PILGRIM'S PROGRESS

A Retelling by
GARY D. SCHMIDT

Illustrated by Barry Moser

WILLIAM B. EERDMANS PUBLISHING COMPANY
GRAND RAPIDS, MICHIGAN

Library of Congress Cataloging-in-Publication Data

Schmidt, Gary D.

Pilgrim's progress : a retelling of John Bunyan's Pilgrim's progress /

by Gary D. Schmidt : [Barry Moser, illustrator].

p.   cm.

Summary: The pilgrim Christian undertakes the

dangerous journey to the Celestial City, experiencing

physical and spiritual obstacles along the way.

ISBN 0-8028-5080-4

[1. Christian life — Fiction.]   I. Moser, Barry, ill.   II. Bunyan, John, 1628-1688.

Pilgrim's progress.   III. Title.

PZ7.S3527P1   1994

[Fic] — dc20   94-8798

                                                                      CIP

                                                                      AC

PREFACE

ON THE DESK NEXT TO ME AS I WRITE this is a black volume printed a century-and-a-half ago across the Atlantic. A thin, frail hand has written on the front page: "For Robert Appleton, with the best wishes of his affectionate mother, Elizabeth Appleton." She wrote that dedication in Boston on New Year's Day, 1844. Below that inscription, dated October 29 of that same year, her son has written of "the laying down of her humanity, that one thing that placed her a little lower than the angels." This book, in which a mother and a son wrote of their love for each other, is an edition of John Bunyan's *Pilgrim's Progress.*

I found this volume in a small house in the Catskill Mountains of New York, in a basement that was so dark I needed a flashlight to read the titles. Among hundreds of mouldering books that no one had read for generations, I found this one, whose gilt lettering still flashed in the light. The binding, worn in spots, was still decorated with a gold filigree that was almost startling in this dark basement. I had never read *Pilgrim's Progress* before, but because you can sometimes judge a book by its cover—not often, but sometimes—I carried this

one out into a daylight it probably had not seen in many years.

That afternoon, in a cool grove of pines, I read John Bunyan's dream, following Christian down a straight and narrow path. Two decades have come and gone since then, but I cannot pass a pine grove without remembering that afternoon. When I open the book beside me even now, I am back in that woods, and back in Bunyan's dream.

Opposite the title page, protected by yellowed tissue paper, is a portrait of Bunyan himself. His clothing is dark and plain. A faint smile, so faint as to be almost unnoticeable, suggests that he thinks this business of portrait painting is rather a fuss. His eyes are focused off to the side, and I can remember thinking that he must have been watching someone—perhaps a child—watching him be painted. And as the painter worked on and the hours passed slowly by, Bunyan must have wanted to tell that child a story. Perhaps it would be a story about patience. Or perhaps it would be about a battle. Or perhaps . . . well, for Bunyan, all of human life was a story, and he could have told about any part of it.

Still, you would not have been able to

guess from his early life that John Bunyan would write stories. He was the son of a Bedfordshire tinker, and he himself grew up intending to make and repair metal pots just as his father did. He had almost no education, and read little. For the first part of his life he was not interested in religious questions, being more occupied with England's civil wars. But after his twenty-fifth birthday he was converted to Christianity and became a preacher.

Bunyan might never have written *Pilgrim's Progress* if he had not opposed England's established church. When he did, he was imprisoned for twelve years. Only then did Bunyan turn to writing. He published his first book, a spiritual autobiography, while he was still in a Bedford jail. When he was released in 1672, however, he immediately began to preach again. For three years he worked at a Bedford church, and if these duties had continued, he would probably not have returned to writing. But in 1675 he was imprisoned again, and in that year he wrote *Pilgrim's Progress* at a desk in his jail cell. This was also the year that the artist came to paint the picture that appears in my volume.

My retelling is not another edition, nor is it just *Pilgrim's Progress* with the language simplified or the lengthy discussions cut out. In this book I have tried to stay close to Bunyan's original but I have attempted to tell his story to a contemporary audience—which is, after all, what he did. Bunyan did not use the high literary styles of his day; instead, he made Christian's journey vivid and exciting by using the most common language of his time. And he depended in large part on images to make his points, images that would be familiar to his readers: fields, rivers, walls, houses, a path. I have tried to do what he did. Perhaps above all I have tried to recapture some of the sense of story that I felt so strongly in the pine woods on a long-ago afternoon.

Anyone who retells a story puts himself or herself into the retelling. So some of the thoughts and reactions of the characters, particularly those of Christian, are my own, though I have tried to keep the characters as Bunyan imagined them, and I have tried to have them respond in ways consistent with Bunyan's understanding of them. The settings are Bunyan's, but colored a bit by settings that I have known or at least imagined.

Bunyan wanted his story to speak to each reader's own experience. This retelling suggests how his story has spoken to mine.

—*Gary D. Schmidt*

PILGRIM'S PROGRESS

THE LIGHTS OF THE HOUSE, THE SHOUTS OF THE *children, the lullaby that my wife was softly cooing, the occasional yips of Jack—all faded as I walked under the velvet sky into the woods. Its paths I knew as well as the road down the valley and into the village. But this one night I missed the straight way and turned onto a path I had not seen before. The branches that laced across it closed behind me as I stumbled on jutting roots and rocks, until soon there was no path to follow.*

So I sat and waited for the moon to rise and light my way home. But instead of the moon, thunderheads came up and winked out the stars one by one. I knew fear, yet I slept.

Listen to the dream that I dreamed that night in the wilderness of the world.

IN THE FIELDS JUST below a small house, a man walked slowly, bent over by the weight of the great pack heaped up over his back and shoulders. The breath of the wind pushed the wheatheads in ripples around him, and every third step seemed to spring a pheasant all aflutter into the air. But the man did not notice. He walked on, holding an open book and turning the pages slowly, slowly.

Beyond him the sun was setting over the western mountains, gilding the sides of the peaks with a light so red that they seemed on fire. When the man saw this, he stepped back, startled. His hands flew to the burden on his shoulders and he cried, "What shall I do?" If he expected an answer, he received none. Nothing changed except the light, which faded to a pale violet. He shuddered and turned back to his house, staggering under the weight of his burden.

"Come inside," called Christiana, his wife, and she stood back as he walked in, shrinking against the doorway so that the pack would not touch her. She peered at the mountains and then quickly closed the door. When she looked in, Christian her husband stood over their children. They stopped their play and watched him silently until Christiana came around and stood between them. "Take off your burden," she said gently. "Take it off and tell me what is so troubling."

It seemed for a moment that he might do it. His hands went to the straps that bound the pack to him, but he could not release the cords. "I'll fetch a knife," volunteered James, but before he could do it, Christian fell under the weight of the burden, and his sorrow rushed out of him.

"We live in the City of Destruction," he wept. "Don't you see the fire on the mountains? It will come upon us too, and I cannot save you." He paused. "I cannot even save myself."

"Hush, hush," soothed Christiana. "It is only the sunset." And she motioned for James and Kathleen to help her lift him.

"No," mumbled Christian, shaking his head. "No." Together Kathleen and James half-carried him to bed, and Rebecca and David brought a heavy quilt, and Jack, his ears down and tail limp, lay beside the bed. But Christian passed that night tossing about, fretted by the pack still tightly strapped to his back.

In the morning Christiana came in and parted the curtains. The sunlight was pouring out of a perfectly blue sky, and Jack, who had not moved the whole night, stood and thumped his tail against the bedside. "Christian," Christiana whispered. "Open your eyes and get up. The world is as it always was. Nothing has happened in the night." But when Christian's eyes opened, they were wild and red.

"No, nothing has changed. The burden is still upon my back. And the light, it is . . ." He trembled and could not finish.

After a sleepless night, Christiana had been so cheered by the cold, clean air of the morning that she had felt sure that Christian too would be changed. Now she grew impatient.

"The burden is there only because you have put it there."

"It is only too true," Christian murmured in response.

"And so you may take it off."

"I cannot," he said, and then he leaned toward her. "What shall I do?"

To this there was no answer, and Christiana left him. She would not speak of the burden anymore, nor would she allow Christian to speak of it to their children, though they stared at it. So he began to spend long hours by himself, taking long walks, reading in his book, thinking about Destruction, weeping for the fate that seemed to hover over his family. Even Jack deserted him.

One day he walked further than usual.

He went eastward, glancing fearfully back over his burden to the mountains that glowered behind him. His burden had grown heavier with the passing days, and the book he read had become more and more distressing. So when he topped a small rise and saw mountains ahead of him, he fell to his knees and shouted to the wind, "What shall I do to be saved?" He did not look up. He did not expect an answer.

But one came.

Along the path ahead of him, Christian saw a man walking briskly. He looked neither young nor old; in fact, he looked no age at all. His beard was white, but his gait was quick, his hands smooth and strong on the staff he carried lightly. He stood quite still when he came up to Christian, and quite straight, waiting for the burdened man to speak. But Christian could hardly hold his head up to look at him, so heavy was the pack.

"Sir," groaned Christian. "Can you help me?"

"Perhaps," nodded the man, and said no more.

"Sir," said Christian, "this book tells me that I will die."

"You hardly need a book to tell you that. Look around you. All things die in the City of Destruction."

"But this burden will sink me lower than the grave."

The man stood quietly, looking around him. Far away he saw Christiana come out of the house, wiping her hands on her apron and looking out toward Christian. "If you already know this," said the man, "why are you standing still?"

Christian paused, and for a moment he held his breath. Then he spoke slowly, daring against all hope to ask the question. "Sir, are you willing to point the way?"

At this the man smiled, and in that smile Christian forgot the terrible weight of his burden. "I am Evangelist. I am willing." He pointed a single finger, unwavering. "Do you see the gate past that second field?"

Christian strained his eyes. "No," he said sadly.

"Your burden must be heavy indeed," said Evangelist. "Do you see a light, at least?"

Again Christian looked hard, and after a time he said, "I think so."

"It is enough for now. Keep it in your eye and run. When you reach the gate, knock."

So Christian began to run. He did not hear the cries of his children, who called after him to return, or look back to see Christiana, who watched him thoughtfully. He did not listen to those neighbors who hurried out to laugh at a man running with a pack on his back. Nor did he hear the pounding footsteps of his friends Obstinate and Pliable until they came up behind him and stopped him by pulling back on his burden.

Obstinate was a burly man with a face

OBSTINATE

squared off at right angles. He liked to cross his arms and hold them high on his chest, and to spread his legs wide as if to give himself a good foundation. Pliable was as thin as the wheat stalks that waved around them, and he was always smiling, though never happy.

"Wait," they urged together. "Come back to Destruction with us, and let's talk about this madness."

"No," said Christian, resuming his pace. "That can never be. Why don't you come away with me instead?"

"And leave our comforts?" Obstinate jeered.

"And our friends?" scoffed Pliable.

"Yes," said Christian simply, stopping to face them. "Leave your comforts and your friends. All together they are not worth more than this one stalk of wheat." He uprooted a stalk and held it out to

PLIABLE

them. His eyes flashed as the wind blew at the wheat seeds until they were all gone. "Come with me and I will prove what I tell you. My book says that we will find joys that never fade."

"Tush on your book," said Obstinate. "Leave him, Pliable. A man who tries to teach a fool is a fool himself."

Pliable had been twisting his hands in front of him and scuffling his feet. "You are right, Obstinate. But Christian is right too. I feel in my heart that I should go with him."

"Tush on your heart," said Obstinate, and turned back.

Pliable watched him go, a little regretfully, it seemed. But when a turn in the road hid him, Pliable looked at Christian cheerfully. "Let's go, then," he said. "And as we walk, perhaps you will tell me more about the place where we are going. Are there shining garments there? And crowns of glory?"

"Yes," said Christian. "And there will be no more sorrow. The Owner of that place shall wipe away any tears. And we will walk with Shining Ones. And our lives will never end. And . . ."

"Let's hurry," Pliable interrupted, as his pace quickened. "I want to have all of this in my hands now." So Pliable began to sprint across the field, with Christian barely keeping up. "Come along," Pliable encouraged.

"I cannot," Christian gasped. "The pack is too heavy, and the ground too marshy."

By now they were approaching the far edge of the second field, and Christian could see the gate shining with a light of its own. But with each step Christian felt the ground grow wetter and softer. The weight of his pack drove his feet deep into a mud that sucked at his ankles. Pliable, who did not seem troubled by the wet ground, paid little attention to Christian's struggles. In his mind he saw himself dressed in a shining robe with a golden crown, until suddenly he felt the ground give way beneath him, and with a cry he and Christian fell into a bog.

It was a place where many had drowned. No animal would go near it; a fox pursued by a pack of hounds would turn to fight rather than plunge into the bog's dark green waters. In Destruction the bog was known as the Slough of Despond, and both Pliable and Christian almost gave up hope as its waters lapped their chins and pushed into their mouths.

"Is this the happiness you promised me?" sputtered Pliable angrily. He was covered with mud and bog water, and his robes were decidedly not shining. A tadpole swam in under his collar, and Pliable's eyes grew wide at the feel of something coiling around his knee.

With a loud yelp he clambered out on the side where he had fallen in. "Tush on your journey," he said. "If this is what we can expect at the beginning, what can we hope for at the end?" He glared back at Christian, wringing the muddy water from his hands and twisting his shoulders. (The tadpole was exploring underneath his cloak.) "Tush!" And he turned and abandoned Christian, who by now was almost completely under the water.

And then Christian did something extraordinary: He pushed out toward the farther side, closer to the Shining Gate. At first he was mostly under water, and his nose and mouth were filled with the stench of the bog. But as he neared the shore, the ground grew surer and surer under him, and his feet did not sink in so deeply. Had he not had the pack on his back, he might have been able to pull himself out. But now, so near the shore, he felt the weight of the pack pushing him under. Pushing him under. Maybe it would be easier . . . to . . . just . . . let . . .

"You there!"

The voice seemed to come from high above him.

"You there! Don't you know that there is a ford to help you cross the bog? Give me your hand." Christian had to will his hand up into the air, and he felt it firmly taken. "Stand up! Stand up, for the love of God!" bellowed the voice.

The words filled Christian with cheer; he felt the ground grow firm under him. He stood up. In front of him was a man with arms like tree trunks, hands as big as shovels, and a chest as round and sturdy as a barrel. His voice seemed to roll around in there until it came out all merry and loud. "I am Help," he said.

"I am Christian."

"And a dreadful mess," laughed Help, clapping Christian on the shoulders. "Fear makes us do terrible things."

"I was not afraid. I was just trying to get across."

Help looked at him with eyes that laughed, but not unkindly. "If you were not afraid, you would have found the ford. This is a place of fear. It wells up from the

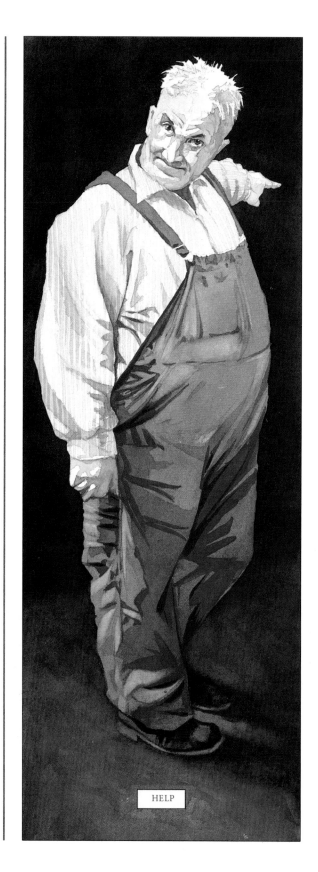

HELP

6

bottom of the bog, like it wells up in our own fearful souls."

Christian shuddered. "I was sent this way by Evangelist."

"So your burden tells me. That is the way you wish to go," said Help, pointing along some firm ground toward the Shining Gate, which now seemed only a short distance away. "Godspeed," Help whispered, and Christian, wiping the slime from his hands, hurried on his way.

Back in Destruction, Christiana looked out her window at the sudden noise in the street. Her neighbors, jeering and laughing, had circled poor, dripping Pliable. Obstinate stood above him, shaking his head and delicately holding a handkerchief to his nose. She turned when her youngest child, David, held out his hands to be picked up. "Such a little one," she cooed as she carried him away from the window, but he had not been interested in the street at all. He pointed to a window that looked over fields to the east.

"Light," he said, pointing with a fist. "Light." But she did not see it.

In my dream I saw a troubled look wrinkle Christiana's face, and I wanted to shout, "Leave your town! Head to the east! Just to go in the right direction would be enough for now!" But as in all dreams I could not do what I most wanted to do.

But then the vision changed, and I saw Christian again. The burden had grown even heavier, and Christian had almost despaired. It seemed that he was ready to do anything to get rid of the pack. Perhaps he was even ready to abandon the path.

II

CHRISTIAN STOPPED ON THE PATH AND strained at the cords that bound the pack to him. They had grown tight with the water of the bog. As soon as he stopped, a man sauntered out from behind a hillock: Mr. Worldly-Wiseman, a short, stout man whose fleshy jowls crowded his

MR. WORLDLY WISEMAN

7

eyes into tiny dots that darted around, taking in and measuring everything he saw. He wore a dark, curly wig and a long velvet frockcoat with gold buttons, and people who did not know him thought that he must be a very important fellow indeed.

"Well, friend," he said in a smooth, cultured voice that rolled its *r*'s, "where are you going, carrying such a large pack?"

Christian pointed ahead of him. "To the Shining Gate, to be relieved of this burden."

"Yes, yes," said Mr. Worldly-Wiseman. "But that gate is still a ways off." He paused, his chin in his hand. "Would you listen to advice if I gave it to you?"

"If it were good advice."

"Yes, yes. Well then, I advise you to get rid of your burden."

Christian sighed. "Evangelist has shown me the way."

"My dear friend. Evangelist is a fine fellow, but if he has pointed you in this direction, you are in for dangers and troubles aplenty. The bog that I can see you have already encountered is only the beginning. Ahead there will be lions and monsters and giants and terror and thirst and hunger." He patted his round belly contentedly. "I would never rush to such things."

"Nor I," said Christian, his face going quite white. "But there is still the burden."

The cords had grown even tighter as they started to dry out.

"Yes, yes, I am coming to that. My advice is this: Put away that book which you have been reading and let me direct you to the village where Mr. Legality lives. There is no one like him for taking burdens off, and his price is . . . well, his price is reasonable. And once your burden is off, you may wish to send for your family and live in that very village. I understand that there are many available houses."

Christian's shoulders hunched under the weight of the pack. "If I . . ."

"There are no 'if's' here, fellow. Make your decision. I am an important man and do not have time to wait upon you." He pulled a silver watch from his vest pocket and glanced at it.

"What is the way to Mr. Legality's house?" asked Christian after a moment.

Mr. Worldly-Wiseman smiled. "Do you see that high hill?"

"Yes, very well."

"His is the first house past that hill." He pulled some papers from inside his coat and walked away.

Christian heaved the pack high on his shoulders and turned toward the high hill. But each step made the pack heavier, the straps tighter. And the mountain seemed to come alive. Boulders tumbled off its slopes and fire gushed out from its crevices, heating the rock so that it glowed red.

Warily, warily he went on, but soon the mountain itself seemed to bend over him, and Christian fell to his knees, regretting that he had ever taken the advice of Mr. Worldly-Wiseman.

"Get up." Christian recognized the voice of Evangelist, and he could not get up because he was ashamed. "Get up!" And now a hand came under Christian's shoulder and helped him rise.

Christian looked into Evangelist's eyes, and he saw that they were flashing and dark. "Weak man of small faith, are you so soon turned out of the way?"

"It was Mr. Worldly-Wiseman who told me to . . ."

"You are the one I find here, not Mr. Worldly-Wiseman. You are the one who listened to the advice of a man who would turn you from the hard but right way, who would offer you treasure now and death later, who would send you to that cheat, Legality, a slave of this mountain that even now bends over you."

Christian knelt down again. "I am lost," he said. "Is there no hope? Can I turn back toward the Gate again?"

"What?" said Evangelist. "To endure lions and monsters and giants, terror and thirst and hunger?"

"If it is the hard but right way, I will hope to endure them all."

Evangelist placed his hand heavily on Christian's shoulder. "So you shall, with God's help and grace. Stand up now and go with the blessing of Emmanuel. Godspeed."

When Christian stood up, Evangelist was gone. He turned his back to the rumblings of the mountain and hurried back the way he had come. He walked quickly, like one going over forbidden ground, where every step is an offense. Having returned to the straight path, he passed many that he knew from neighboring villages who called to him, but he would not listen. He passed Mr. Worldly-Wiseman, who blustered, "And is this, then, the upshot of my advice?" But Christian did not even look at him, and soon he had left them all behind.

And then he was at the Shining Gate.

The Gate was as high and solid and formidable as any that Christian had ever seen. It stood in granite walls where the stones were so well fitted that there were no seams. Above it was a shining beacon, but the iron bands that held the Gate's timbers were black, and the hinges seemed so solid that it was hard to imagine that they ever moved. Christian reached out to feel the door, as if to test the weight of the wood, but he drew his hand back quickly. The door was covered with old bloodstains.

"How in . . ." he began, but an arrow flew by his left shoulder and buried its head in the door. Another thudded into

the spot where his hand had been only a moment before. As much as the pack would allow him, he crouched and looked around. There on a high plateau, mostly hidden by a broiling yellow fog, he was able to pick out the outlines of turrets. The wind brought a confused babble to his ears, the sounds of shouts and commands.

Christian pounded on the door. "Open the Gate! Open the Gate!"

A solemn voice answered, "Who is it that calls for the Shining Gate to open?"

"A poor soul from the City of Destruction, following the teaching of Evangelist." Another arrow flew past Christian's shoulder.

The door opened almost immediately. Despite its massive size, it moved easily and with no sound. A hand reached out, grabbed Christian's forearm, pulled him inside, and closed the door again. The puck, puck of arrows hitting the door continued for a minute, then faded away.

Christian could hardly find his voice. "Thank you, sir," he whispered. "You have saved me."

By now the sun had dipped below the world's edge and the sky was violet. In the east it was already quite dark. High on the ramparts above the Gate, someone was playing a trumpet so gladly that it seemed as if the highest notes were glittering the sky with stars. People heard it back in the City of Destruction, but no one, ex-

cept perhaps Christian's daughter Rebecca, knew what the playing was for.

"I am Goodwill," the porter announced to Christian, "and always ready to open

GOODWILL

the Gate with all my heart. The arrows of Beelzebub are sharp and deadly, and many have been killed at the Gate even as they were about to knock." Christian shuddered, remembering the dark stains.

"It is all right to shudder at what is past," Goodwill said. "But that is over now. Look ahead. The Shining Gate has been opened to you, and no one can shut it."

"So it is as Evangelist said?"

Goodwill smiled and took him by the hand. "Did you ever doubt it?"

Christian nodded gravely. "Yes. When I almost drowned in the Slough of Despond. And when I left the path to find Mr. Legality."

"His mountain has been the death of many, and it will be the death of many more. You are fortunate to have escaped." Christian nodded. "But were you all alone? Did no one else follow?"

"No one but Obstinate and Pliable."

"But they are not with you now."

"No."

"And your family?"

"Nor my family."

They walked for a time in silence, each thinking his own thoughts. The path came straight out from the Gate, so straight that it seemed to shoulder trees and hills and even streams out of its way. The early evening stars were now fully out, and Christian could not help but think of walks he had taken with Christiana and his children through the valley under those very same skies.

"All shall be well," said Goodwill.

Christian looked at Goodwill, startled. Had Goodwill been able to read his thoughts? And then the reply came into his mind: "And all shall be well," he said.

"And all manner of things shall be well." Goodwill paused. "Now Christian, follow the path. Keep to the straight way. Do not stray to the right or to the left."

"But if I . . ."

"Whenever you must choose, take the straight and narrow way."

"The hard but right way," said Christian. "I remember. And my burden?"

"If I could, I would remove it from you."

Christian understood then that Goodwill could do nothing to relieve his burden. He sighed once, then hefted the pack high up on his shoulders. "Then I shall keep on," he said.

Goodwill said nothing. He pointed down the path, waved, and walked back to tend the Gate. He would not have to wait long before another knock would come.

For Christian it had been a day like no other. Only that morning he had been walking in fields he had known since he was a boy. But now! Now he was on a path he had never known before; he had never even heard of it! In his right hand he still held the book he had been reading, and he opened it again and read until the fading light made reading impossible. Still he walked on, now very weary and hardly able to hold the pack up. When he saw a large house with merrily lit windows, he stumbled to it and knocked upon the door.

No answer.

Christian knocked again.

No answer.

Suddenly Christian heard a ferocious dog barking madly. The sound seemed to come from far away, yet at the same time it seemed close. He knocked yet again, and this time the door opened and Christian fell into a lighted hall. Sleep overtook him, and he hardly felt the tender hands that picked him up as lightly as a baby and carried him to a quilted bed.

Christian woke early, confident that he was on the right way, but anxious to begin his journey again. Through the early dawn hours he watched the wheeling stars, until little by little the sky turned grey, then pink, and the stars faded back beyond sight. He sat up to watch the sun peer over the horizon, and when it came, a great chorus of birds, silent until then, burst into such a cackling and chirruping and whistling that it seemed to Christian that they had never seen a dawn before.

"A new miracle every day, no less a miracle because it is expected."

Christian turned at the voice; he had not heard anyone come into the room. He could not find words to describe what the speaker looked like, and whenever he was asked about him afterward, Christian could never quite describe what he saw. "There was a kind of full gladness about him," he would say, "but he was more than glad. He was so very, very sure." He remembered nothing of how he looked.

"I am the Interpreter," the man said, "and I have some things to show you which might be of profit to you." Without waiting for Christian to reply, he turned and opened the door to the hallway, the breeze from it flickering the candle he held and dancing shadows on the wall.

Christian followed the Interpreter down a long, well-lighted hall. On either side were doors that opened into rooms equally well-lighted, but they did not enter them all. The first one they went into was bracingly cold, so that Christian, who had stifled a yawn in the hall, was suddenly wide awake. On the wall was a picture of a man who looked up to heaven. In his hand he held the book that Christian himself carried, and a golden crown set with gems hung above his head. Behind his back—and here Christian peered more closely—was a long, narrow path. Christian thought he could pick out the Gate, the mountain of Mr. Legality, the Slough of Despond, even his own village.

"What does this mean?" Christian asked.

"The man you see," answered the Interpreter, "has turned from the things of the world to the things of heaven, and so he looks to the promise of glory." He paused as Christian looked back to the picture. "Everything I show you is for you to remember, to help you when you must choose between the easy way . . ."

"And the hard but right way," Christian finished.

The Interpreter smiled and led him to

the next room. Here a young girl was sweeping, but the dust was so thick and so dry that she was only stirring it into the air. "Sprinkle the room with water," suggested the Interpreter. This the young girl did, and soon the dust had come out of the air and lay swept up in heaps.

"The dust," said the Interpreter, "is sin. The first sweeping was that of the law; it did not dispel sin, but only made it more obvious."

"I know the lesson well," said Christian, remembering the mountain of Mr. Legality.

"But the second sweeping was that of grace, which cleans the room as it revives the soul."

In another chamber a fire blazed hotly, filling the room with a cheering heat. A man with a pitcher stood near the fire, splashing the logs with water. But the fire did not even sputter.

"How can this be?" asked Christian.

"Come around to the back side of the wall," answered the Interpreter. There they found another man secretly pouring oil on the flames. "The man in front," explained the Interpreter, "is the devil, trying to put out the fire, which is the work of grace. The man behind is Christ, who in quietness and stillness encourages the work already begun in the heart."

Christian nodded gravely.

"I have two more rooms to show you. The next is to make you fear." They en-

tered a high, dark room with bare floors and no windows. A single gloomy candle lit one corner, throwing a sickly yellow light on a figure crouched sullenly in an iron cage.

"Interpreter, who is this man?"

"Who is this man, you ask," came a thin voice from inside the cage. "Who is

DESPAIR

this man? I could be anyone. I could even be you. But I am myself: Despair." The speaker paused and nodded his head—sadly, it seemed to Christian. "I was once like you, headed to the Celestial City. But I lost the way and turned to another. And now I am eternally lost, imprisoned in this iron."

"Is there no way to come out?"

"None."

"Could you not repent and turn again to the right way?"

"No."

"Could you . . ."

"Leave me alone. Must you plague me with your possibilities? I am Despair, and I am lost."

Christian and the Interpreter left the room quietly and not a little sadly. "Is there no hope for him?" asked Christian.

"One," said the Interpreter.

Before Christian could ask what that one hope might be, a man in bright silver armor marched past them and down the

SHINING KNIGHT

hall. Beside one of the doors a group of people sat, wringing their hands, taking a step forward and then springing back. Christian had not noticed them before. A man sat behind a desk in front of the door, holding a pen poised above a lined book. He was to take down the names of all those who wished to enter. Behind him and just inside the door, a group of dark knights stood sternly, holding their swords and pikes before them. Everyone who waited outside was afraid to go past them.

The shining knight strode up to the man at the desk. "Put down my name," he said resolutely, and without waiting he drew his sword and rushed upon the dark knights.

The clash of their meeting was louder than Christian could ever have imagined. The knight slashed at the heads of the pikes leveled against his chest. With his right hand he held back one of the dark ones who clutched a long dagger, while striking another with the pommel of his sword. Leaping over a jab at his knees, he pushed himself past the knights, wounded but still strong.

Christian smiled. "I think I know the meaning of this."

"Yes," said the Interpreter, "I think you do."

"Am I to see behind any of the other doors, sir?"

"No."

"Are there no more lessons to be learned?"

The Interpreter held Christian's elbow. "Many more to be learned, but all of the doors are not for you. Some are for those who will come after. And perhaps

15

now there is a lesson of a different kind to be learned."

They went downstairs together to a stone kitchen. The whitewashed walls gleamed back the warmth and merriment of the fire. The slight wood smell blended with that of baked bread, and a large breakfast was set on a rough wooden table. The food was plain and good, just the kind you would want for a long journey.

Afterward, when they had finished, Christian and the Interpreter went outside. Christian looked ahead at the path. It was rough, but straight. A high wall as sure as salvation ran alongside the path, and Christian was eager to begin, despite his heavy burden.

The Interpreter raised his hand in a blessing: "The Comforter always be with you, Christian, to guide you to the City." And so Christian took his leave and turned to the path. He did not ask if the Interpreter could relieve his burden. He knew that that time would come when it would come.

And though he did not know it, that time was upon him.

He came to the bottom of a steep hill where a dark tomb gaped open at one side. He began to climb the hill, but it grew steeper and steeper, so that soon he was crawling. With perhaps the last of his strength, he reached the top and looked up. There before him stood a Cross, the

sun, now fully up, shining splendidly on its dark wood.

The straps of the burden loosed, the knots unraveled, the pack shifted weight, and then it rolled off. It fell to the ground and crashed down the hill, rolling faster and faster until it tumbled into the mouth of the open tomb. Christian never saw it again.

In my dream I saw the burden lifted from Christian's shoulders and watched it tumble into darkness. I was filled with an unaccountable joy, as though it had fallen from my own shoulders, and I wanted to do something. To sing, perhaps. Or run. Or twirl about, my arms out to gather sunlight.

It was only the beginning of the journey, but it was a good beginning. For both of us.

III

CHRISTIAN STOOD ASTOUNDED. HE reached up to feel behind him. There was nothing there. He reached up over his shoulders. Nothing. The burden was gone, totally gone. With a wild yell he leapt up, as lightly, it seemed, as if the air itself bore

him. He felt behind him again, and a song burst from him, a song he remembered from his childhood, a song full of love and gratitude. He fell to his knees and then rolled in the green grass of the hill, weeping and laughing to have the burden gone. Then he lay on his back, clutching the grass in his hands, smelling the sweet herbal scent in the air (he must have rolled over some thyme), and looked deep into the blue of the sky. It had been a long time since he had seen it so blue.

"Peace be with you," came a voice. Christian looked up, too happy to be ashamed of being found rolling in the grass and crying.

"And with you," Christian said automatically. (How do I remember that answer? he wondered.) Three Shining Ones stood before him, their feet not bending the blades of grass. They moved with such delicacy, as if they were treading lightly on the world that rolled underneath them.

"Your sins are forgiven, your burden gone," said the first. Christian looked at the Cross. He had known this was so.

The second stripped off Christian's clothes, ripped by the cords of the pack and stained by the waters of the Slough, and dressed him in new, sturdy clothes.

The third kissed Christian on the forehead as he handed him a rolled parchment, closed with a red wax seal im-

printed with the sign of the Owner. "Keep this close to you until you arrive at the Celestial City," he said.

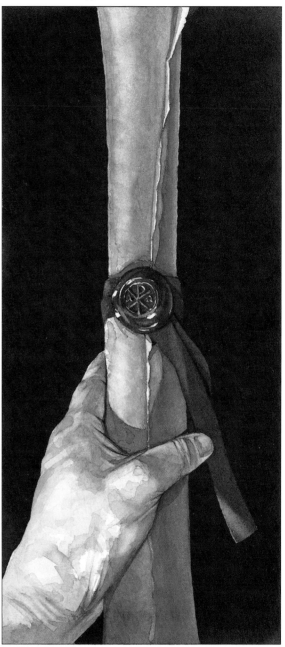

Then all three turned and pointed down the hill along the straight path. Christian looked at them—What can one give to grace?—and bounded down the hill, running so quickly now that he was free of the burden.

But at the bottom of the hill, he came upon three men whose feet were held fast by chains. They were asleep, and Christian felt that they must have fallen into sleep exhausted by attempts to free

SIMPLE

themselves. "Wake up!" he urged loudly, kneeling down to examine the chains. "Don't give up now, not when you are so close to this hill especially. I'll help you."

The three looked up, yawned, and rubbed their eyes sleepily. "Who is this fellow?" said Simple to the two others. "He wakes us up as if there were some danger about." He spoke slowly, as though his words too were sleepy.

"But there is!" cried Christian.

"Then let us rest and prepare for it,"

said Sloth, and he and Simple turned over and began to snore.

"Can I not at least help you?" asked Christian of the third.

"Every tub must stand upon its own bottom," replied Presumption, and smiling at his own wit, he yawned twice,

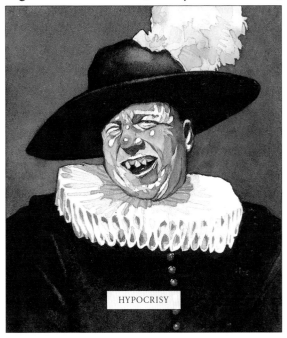

HYPOCRISY

stretched, closed his eyes, and went back to sleep.

"How strange," Christian thought aloud, walking on. He held the parchment tightly. "Am I the only one willing to take this path?"

"Hardly, good sir!" The voice came from a rather fat man clambering over the wall that ran beside the path. He was accompanied by a tall, thin fellow with a sallow face and an unhappy expression. If he had ever smiled, it had been a long time ago.

"My name is Hypocrisy," said the large man, wiping at the sweat that ran over his jowls and adjusting his waistcoat. He reached into his pocket and pulled out a pinch of snuff. "And this," he pointed at his companion, "is Formalist."

Formalist bowed low and said nothing.

"Well met, gentlemen," replied Christian. "But how is it that you come in over the wall instead of through the Shining Gate?"

"We come from the land of Vainglory, and as everyone in our country knows, it is much too far for us to go round about to the Gate, when we have such an admirable shortcut here over the wall."

"But that is not how the Owner rules it."

"Well, fellow," said Hypocrisy, not a little annoyed. "Tush." (Where had Christian heard that word before?) "You are here on the path, and so are we. Perhaps you did come through the Gate. Perhaps not. In any case, how is your condition now any different from ours?"

Formalist spoke for the first time. "If we are here, we are here. If the conditions are the same, then it's all the same."

Hypocrisy nodded. "Quite so, quite so. Now let us walk on to the Celestial City, and let each man look to himself."

"But you have no Rolls."

"There is no doubt that when the time comes, we shall have what we need. Tush, man, do you think that fellows such as we,

who have come in with all good intentions, should be turned away at the last? Such pride, such arrogance ill befit you."

The three walked on, Christian slightly ahead and reading in his Roll, the other two remarking on the dustiness of the path.

After a time they came to a fork in the path. To the left and to the right the path broadened out. Both side roads were softened by banks of moss and lined with aspens, their leaves quivering in the breeze. Both beckoned. Ahead, the path narrowed. It grew steeper and steeper as it climbed into a mountain called Difficulty. The three men could see that it wound far above the tree line, and that whoever climbed it would be dangerously exposed.

Christian stuffed the parchment into his shirt and began to climb. "Are you mad?" scorned Hypocrisy. "Do you not see these two other roads?"

"The way ahead is the hard but right way."

"There are many ways to the Celestial City," intoned Formalist, "for many are called."

"So it is," agreed Hypocrisy. "Formalist, I shall take the left, and you the right. We shall meet again on the far side of this mountain, and leave this madman to his climb."

Formalist nodded gravely and set off. Hypocrisy looked once at Christian and

then turned to his road. Neither had gone far before he was in a dark wood. No one knows what happened to them there, but they were never seen again.

Though Christian started up the mountain briskly, he soon found that his legs were growing weaker and his knees tired. At times he would clamber over rough rocks, buffeted by the cold winds that fell down off the mountain. Soon most of the trees were gone, and though the sunlight shone on him, it gave no warmth.

Before long the path was merely the least rough place in a blasted mountainside. Much of the way Christian crawled, but often he had to haul himself up rocks that had almost no foothold. Twice he had to leap over wide chasms, and once he had to shimmy along a ledge no wider than his foot. If it had not been for the promises in his Roll, he might have given up and returned to the broad roads.

Almost three-quarters of the way up the mountain, where there were only a few trees stunted and gnarled by the chilling winds, Christian found an arbor set in a sunny, enclosed place, planted long ago by the Owner for travelers to the Celestial City. It was a place meant for brief respite only, but as the sun laid its gentle hands upon Christian's shoulders and the trees spread green shadows in front of him, his eyes grew heavy, his breathing deeper. "I should rest to prepare for the hardships ahead," he thought, and finally the weariness of the climb lured him to sleep. And as he slept, the Roll fell out from under his shirt.

It was almost evening when he woke up, the sun a deep red. In the west the first stars were already out, but Christian decided to finish his climb. He had almost reached the top of the mountain when he met two men, who were hastily climbing down toward him. At first he thought they might be Hypocrisy and Formalist, but

TIMOROUS AND MISTRUST

both of these men were smaller. They walked hunched together, their heads darting fitfully from side to side.

"But you're going the wrong way!" Christian called.

"Wrong way?" cried the one named Timorous. "Ahead there are lions and demons and all sorts of dangers. We are not the ones going the wrong way."

"But surely the Owner of this place will guard us from . . ."

"From nothing," finished the other, named Mistrust. "If the lions had not been sleeping, we would have been torn to pieces. Come with us now, before it is too late. There is nothing for you ahead."

Christian thought for a moment. "There is nothing for me behind. If I go back to Destruction, I will perish there."

Mistrust and Timorous shrugged their shoulders. "We will tell your wife that you died bravely, though foolishly," Timorous said, and they set off down the mountain.

Christian watched them go and then looked back up the path. It was almost completely dark now, and he wondered if he would be able to see the lions. He felt in his shirt to be comforted by the promises of the Roll—but it was gone.

"Fool!" he cried, looking around wildly. "Where could I have dropped it?" He searched all around, and then, almost weeping with frustration, he began to climb back down the way he had come, going slowly so that he would not miss the Roll in the darkness. He had to go all the way back to the arbor, and there it lay, where he had slept.

"Fool!" he said again. "I might have

been far along by this time, but I slept and wasted all the afternoon."

Even so, the arbor looked so peaceful, so quiet under the stars that Christian was tempted to stay there that night. But when he looked back up the path and realized how far he had to go, he set out again, feeling with his hands and feet for the right holds, since the dark was so deep that it was almost impossible to see.

When he reached the point where he had met Mistrust and Timorous, he began to think again of the lions. "What should I do?" he wondered. "Night is the time they prowl about." He climbed slowly upward, and when he finally reached the top of the mountain, he looked over to the far side and saw, not far from him, a stately palace—the Palace Beautiful. A bright light spread up its walls, up onto the pointed towers, and finally caught the underside of the banners that fluttered bravely in the night air. Perhaps there he could get safe lodging.

He started down the path, then stood as one made of stone. Was that a low growling he had heard? The wind moaning among the rocks made it difficult to be sure.

But two more steps made Christian quite sure.

A terrific roar rolled up from the Palace, quickly followed by another. Christian held his Roll tightly and walked ahead, feeling that he was the only creature who could not see clearly in this dark night. The trees seemed to close in behind him and push him ahead. Still he could not see.

But then suddenly, so close to the Palace that he could see its open door, he found himself upon the lions. They had quieted at his approach, waiting for him to come to them, and now they both sprang, jaws wide open, claws fully extended, ears laid flat. The clash of iron chains made Christian only more afraid, and he started back.

Then three things happened at the same time. The lions stopped. A porter came out of the open door of the Palace. And the moon suddenly sprang up into the sky, so full of light it seemed to drip it from overflowing. The path glowed in the milky light, straight and narrow to the door.

"Is your strength so small?" called the porter, whose name was Watchful. "The lions are chained; do not fear them. Try your faith, man. Walk in the center of the path and nothing will harm you."

Christian looked behind him, and then looked again at the lions, who had scuttled back out of the moonlight and now crouched in the shadows, glaring at him with reddened eyes. All creation was absolutely quiet. It waited.

"Come," encouraged Watchful.

Christian came. He held his Roll tightly, but trembled as he drew close to the lions. They sprang at him again, but Christian forced himself on, straight down the milk-white path, straight toward the open door. The hot breath of the lions chilled his neck, but he kept on. Their claws reached toward his shoulders, but he kept on. And when he had passed the lions, he clapped his hands and smiled broadly.

Watchful came down the steps and held his hand out to Christian, who grasped it joyfully. "Welcome to the Palace Beautiful," Watchful said.

Christian found it hard to speak, but after a moment he asked, "May I lodge in this house tonight?"

"We do not usually open the doors to one who comes so late. Where did you spend last night?"

"At the Interpreter's House."

"Yet you come here so late now?" Christian sighed and told the porter sadly of the arbor and how he lost the Roll. Watchful nodded as he listened.

"It is a tale I have heard before, though not often with such a happy ending. Come inside now, and I will bring you to the ladies of this palace."

So Watchful brought in Christian. The hall was high-ceilinged and large. Their feet clicked against a bright tile mosaic on the floor, but the sound was caught and muffled by the tapestries whose silver and gold threads shimmered on the walls.

They walked through into a second room, smaller and perhaps more comfortable than the first, though equally rich. In the middle of this room stood a tall, dignified lady dressed in a long white robe tied with a crimson belt. She seemed just to have stood to greet them, and she came forward slowly, hand extended, not wasting a single movement.

"What is your name?" she asked, looking into Christian's eyes.

"Christian," he replied, "a pilgrim from the City of Destruction." Without her asking, Christian began to tell her his story, and by the time he was finished, tears stood in her eyes.

"You are welcome here," she said quietly. "This house was built by the Owner, Emmanuel, for the relief of pilgrims such as you." With a nod she sent Watchful to call her sisters, and she sat back down on a wooden chair stained darkly, indicating another place for him to sit. "My name is Discretion," she said. "And now let us talk of your journey, and of what you have faced and overcome."

"You seem very sure of me, my lady," said Christian.

Discretion smiled, and they talked long before her three sisters came into the room. Then she and Christian, together with Prudence, Charity, and Piety, went into another room where Watchful had prepared a full table of fruits and cheeses

on white plates, dark red wine in silver goblets, and baskets of warm rolls.

Christian could have stayed there a long time. He talked about the way he had come and of his family. The sisters encouraged him to continue to follow the hard but right way, and though they would not tell him what soon lay ahead,

DISCRETION

they promised him a gift in the morning that would help him in his journey.

Then they told him about the Owner of the Palace Beautiful, of how He was a great warrior who had fought with and overcome the one who held the power

of death. He was a lover of pilgrims, the sisters agreed, who wanted all to come to Him in the Celestial City, where He received worthy pilgrims with a joy so strong and so complete that it could not be known outside of that city.

By the time they had finished, it was very late. Christian had lost his weariness in the Palace, but when he was led to an upper chamber, and when he lay down under the thick covers and watched the firelight flicker on the walls, and when he looked out the eastern window and saw the firefolk glistening brightly against the dark, he grew content and still, and at last fell asleep. The lions were quiet. Their chains were unmoving. Christian was in a chamber called Peace, and he slept that night more soundly than any night since he had been a child.

If he had known what the next day would bring, he would not have slept so soundly.

In my dream I trembled. Christian had come so far and had overcome so much. But why would Discretion not speak of what lay ahead of him? And why were the lions so quiet?

As I watched, the eastern sky paled, then

reddened. It threw a rosy glow into the chamber called Peace, and though Christian was not yet awake, it seemed that he too felt it, for he smiled.

Would he be as cheerful when the sun set that night? I trembled again, though I did not know why.

IV

WHEN CHRISTIAN CAME DOWN IN THE morning, Watchful was waiting for him. They were to go to the Armory, Watchful said, where the four sisters would be waiting. They went quickly through long halls richly carpeted, lit by tall, many-paned windows. Had Christian gone alone, he would have become quickly turned around, but with Watchful he was soon at the stout oak door that guarded the Armory. The wood was old and strong.

"But it seems slashed and hacked at," observed Christian.

"Much of what you see inside has been slashed and hacked at," answered Watchful. "This is, after all, the stuff of war."

The first thing Christian saw inside was Discretion and her three sisters, standing quite straight and quite still. It was the kind of room where you wanted to be quiet, like an old church that makes you whisper in the half-light. The dark

rafters leapt across the ceiling from one wall to the other, and from them hung bright banners depicting the stories of pilgrims to the Celestial City. (Many banners were yet blank.) On the walls hung shields and breastplates and helmets, and stacked beneath them were leggings and mailed gloves. Some of the armor was bright and new, but much of it was dented in many places and stained by old wounds.

Prudence walked to the wall and lifted off a breastplate. She brought it to Christian and strapped it on him. "To protect you against the one who wields death," she said.

Next, Piety fitted on a helmet and leggings. "So that you may be strong in the battles before you."

Charity gave him a broadsword. Gold embroidery twisted around its hilt, and the tempered blade felt cool to the touch.

Discretion brought a great round shield. "To avert the darts of the wicked one," she said quietly.

Finally the sisters fitted him with a pair of gloves. He stood before them, overcome by the greatness of their gift. But there was one problem.

"I have no armor for my back," he said.

"Do you intend to retreat and show your back to your enemies?" asked Discretion.

Then Christian understood. "No, my

CHARITY'S GIFT

lady," he said, smiling sheepishly. "I have no need of such armor."

"Then come," Discretion said. "We have one more thing to show you before you must be off."

They brought him up long stairways to the highest turret in the Palace. When Christian looked down, he saw birds flying far beneath him, and silvery brooks glinted back the sun. "Look to the south," said Discretion, pointing. There, far away, pleasant blue mountains balanced on the plains, decorated with spring-green woods and vineyards just leafing out.

Down the mountains flowed bright water from springs and fountains, and along their banks crowded great masses of red and purple and white flowers.

"That is Emmanuel's Land, the Delectable Mountains," said Discretion, "and from the very top of those mountains you can glimpse the gates of the Celestial City."

Christian was overcome with the desire to set out immediately, and he bounded down the stairs so quickly that the four sisters could not keep up with him. When he reached the bottom, he waited for them, pacing. They came down smiling; they understood his impatience better than he did himself. So with few goodbyes but much gratitude, Christian set off.

"Farewell, Watchful," called Christian to the porter standing outside. "Emmanuel be with you for all the kindness you have shown to me."

"Godspeed, Christian," returned Watchful. "If you hurry, you may catch a pilgrim who passed by not long ago."

"His name?" asked Christian.

"Faithful."

"I know him! He was my neighbor in the City of Destruction. So he too has come out!"

"Yes," said the porter. "He would be a good friend to accompany you. And you will have need of such friends. You have overcome the mountain called Difficulty, but now you descend to the low places, the

28

deep Valley of Humiliation. Go with Emmanuel." Watchful handed Christian a sack with a loaf of bread, a bottle of wine, and a cluster of raisins, and waved him down the trail.

Christian went carefully down the hill and then into a dark valley. He was eager to find his way to the mountains he had seen, but the words of Watchful had made him uneasy.

By the middle of the morning, Christian was well into the valley. The high hills above him hid the sun, yet though there was little light, the ground beneath him was quite warm, and often he would pass rocks that glowed dully. Nothing living grew there. There was no breeze. There was no sound but the grinding of chipped pebbles under Christian's feet. Everything else seemed perfectly still.

Christian's hand went down to his sword. He had not heard anything, but he felt . . . And then he did hear something. It was the sound of something huge, monstrously huge, and its paces trembled the earth.

Christian stood firm. He had no armor for his back.

The thing came on, and then it was before him. The rocks it touched on its way glowed, and by their light Christian saw the creature. The scales on its chest shone redly, and its great wings seemed to fan the scales into greater heat. Its hands and feet were clawed like a bear's, its mouth fitted with teeth like a lion's. Its belly was opened by a second, hideous mouth, spewing fire and smoke. It breathed its name: Apollyon.

"Where are you from?" slowly groaned the monster, and Christian could not tell which mouth spoke the words.

He stood transfixed, his hand gripping his sword. He could not answer.

"Where are you from?" repeated the monster, advancing one step closer.

Then Christian remembered the Palace Beautiful, and he felt the Roll pressed against his chest. He drew his sword and held it out in front of him.

"Monster," he called, "I come from the City of Destruction. I am on my way to the Celestial City. Come no further near me."

"Come no further?" questioned Apollyon. "Come no further? One of my own subjects commands me?"

"I am no subject of yours."

"I own the City of Destruction. All its citizens are my subjects. How is it that you have run from my domain?" Fire breathed out of its belly. "If I did not expect more service from you soon, I would blast you to a cinder now."

"I was born into your country and into your hard service. But I am become a pilgrim now. I have met Evangelist, who has shown me . . ."

"Enough!" Apollyon's eyes glowed terribly at the name of Evangelist. Fire belched again from its lower mouth, but it paused to control itself. "Well," it said, in a sweetened voice, "I do not wish to lose my subjects so lightly. Return to Destruction, and I promise to make your service easy. You will receive whatever my country can give you."

"I am pledged to another, and I cannot go back now."

"Many have pledged to Emmanuel and then returned to my service. You found it easy to leave one lord; you will find it easy to leave another."

"No," said Christian, still holding his sword before him. "I like His service better, and His government, and His servants, and His country. You can offer me nothing. I am no longer your servant. Come no further!"

"His servants often do not come to a good end," gloated Apollyon. He fingered the fiery spears that he held in his left hand. "Many have never left this valley." Christian made no answer but to hold his shield before him.

"And after all, how do you know He will have you as His servant? You have proved traitor to your first lord, and already you have been disloyal to your second."

"When, Apollyon, have I been unfaithful to Him?"

Apollyon leered and came another step closer. "When you almost failed in the Slough of Despond. When you tried disloyal ways of removing your burden. When you almost turned back at the sight of the lions. When you took pride in telling of your so-called victories at the Palace Beautiful."

"All this is true," admitted Christian, "and much more that you have left out. But the prince that I serve is merciful and ready to forgive."

Apollyon beat its wings and rose up into the air, screeching so loudly that the valley shook. "I am the enemy of Emmanuel," it bellowed. "I hate Him and His laws and His country." It landed directly in front of Christian, crashing down so hard that it split the ground. "But most of all," the monster hissed, "I hate His pilgrims. Beware! Go back now and serve me."

Christian stood firm. "I am on the King's Way of Holiness. To serve you would be death."

"Then," said Apollyon, holding a flaming spear over its shoulder, "I swear by my infernal den that I will spill your soul." It had hardly finished speaking before it threw the spear directly at Christian's heart. Christian parried with his shield, but the heat and force of the monster's throw drove him back.

Straddling the path, Apollyon threw spear after spear at Christian. They came so fast that Christian could not close with the monster, and soon he was wounded

across his forehead and in his left hand and foot. The wounds burned, and Christian found himself growing weaker. Apollyon, sensing the victory, moved closer, throwing more and more spears, so that soon Christian could barely hold his shield up, so weakened was his arm.

For half a day they fought, Christian little by little giving ground, the monster moving closer and closer, the spears coming harder and harder. Christian was almost overcome by the stench that blew from Apollyon's wings, and as the blood from his forehead ran into his eyes, he could barely see well enough to parry the spears. And still he had not even come close to wounding his foe.

As Christian took yet another step backward, Apollyon flew into the air and landed hard on the ground in front of him, throwing him off balance. Apollyon moved even closer and with a great sweep of its wings buffeted Christian to the ground, skittering away his sword.

Apollyon screeched with triumph, and fire scorched out of its belly. "Now, traitorous pilgrim, you receive the wages of your disloyalty!" The monster flew up again and this time landed atop the fallen Christian. It screeched once, raised its clawed hand, and hurtled it toward Christian's face.

But at that moment, as Emmanuel would have it, Christian reached out and caught his sword. With its arm raised up, Apollyon had exposed its side, and Christian thrust his sword deep, deep into the monster. "We are more than conquerors," Christian yelled, "through Him who loves us!" With a hideous yell of horror and pain, the monster jolted back, leaving the sword in Christian's hand covered with black blood. Clutching its right side, it screeched twice. And then, one wing hanging limply, it lunged away into the darkness, hissing and screeching to the black sky.

It was the most dreadful battle Christian had ever seen. He stood up, shaky and staggering. He was covered with his own blood as well as Apollyon's. But as he watched the creature scuttle away, he smiled. Another song came to his mind, and in the midst of all the darkness of the valley, he sang it:

To Him let me give lasting praise,
And thank and bless His name always.

Perhaps it was the defeat of Apollyon, or perhaps it was the song itself, but as soon as Christian finished, a beam of light shot through the darkness of the valley. It lit a large tree by the path, a tree so strong and lush and fertile that even this valley could not kill it. It was the Tree of Life, miraculously sprung to life in this barren place, and Christian used

its leaves to stop his bleeding and to heal his grievous wounds. He sat under it, bathed in that potent sunlight, and ate his bread and drank his wine. And then he stood, strong again, holding his sword out in front of him, because he did not know if there was any other enemy like Apollyon at hand.

There was not.

There were worse enemies.

At the end of the Valley of Humiliation lay another valley, the Valley of the Shadow of Death. If Apollyon's valley was dark, this one was black. The path that stretched ahead of him was treacherously dark. The trees in the valley had all died from the poisonous ground. Any rainwater that fell there was instantly poisoned as it sank to their roots. The wind that blew through that place was hot and sick, and it carried moanings and groanings so terrible that no man could make

them. Nothing lived there but creatures that have no name.

Christian stood at the entrance to that dark place, still holding his sword in front of him. "In the name of Emmanuel," he called boldly, his voice quivering just a little, "I . . ."

He was interrupted by terrified cries. Two men came stumbling through the underbrush, falling over themselves in their haste.

"Is that a human voice?" cried one.

"Back, back!" shouted the other.

"Stand and tell me what you are running from," commanded Christian. One rushed away, his face white and his eyes rounded with fear. But the other paused, gasping for breath.

"We were almost into the valley, and what we saw would make anyone's blood turn to ice. Hobgoblins, satyrs, ghouls, and demons flutter around damned souls, bound in iron and groaning so loudly that the stones crack. Clouds of dark confusion hang over the whole valley, and above those broods Death itself, spreading its awful wings."

"But if this is the only way to the Celestial City, what choice do we have but to go through it?"

The man did not answer but made his choice by running after his companion. After a moment and a deep breath, Christian went on ahead.

Within three steps the path became so narrow that it was barely the width of his foot. Still holding his sword out in front of him, he struggled for his balance. And well he might, for on his right there was a sheer drop. He could not see the bottom, but when he dislodged a stone, it was a fearfully long time before he heard it strike the ground below. On his left, the dark green waters of a swamp lapped just below the level of the path. No one who had ever fallen into it had ever come out again. Christian moved slowly. It was so dark that, once he had lifted up his foot to take a step forward, he did not know where, or upon what, he would set it down again.

Afterward, he could never tell how long he had been on the path. He seemed to struggle along the first part of it for many hours. He remembered the darkness growing deeper, the heat becoming more intense. But these were nothing compared with the great horror of that place.

He came to it about midway on the path. It was the mouth of hell itself, filled with a terrible fire that gave off no light but a foul smoke, so that Christian could only breathe in short gasps. The wails of demons high in the air above him chilled his skin, and he shivered in spite of the heat.

Terrified and uncertain, he stopped.

For a moment he thought he might turn back. Voices in his ears whispered that he was a fool to go forward, that he would surely die, that the path led to hell and not at all to the Celestial City. And when he

heard a great company of demons coming toward him, he took a step backward.

If at that moment Christian had turned his back, the demons would have ripped him to shreds. But Christian did not turn his back. He saw that his sword was of no use against enemies such as these. Sheathing it, he stepped forward into the very middle of the demons. "I will walk in the strength of the Lord God!" he shouted, then walked sternly ahead. The

demons gave way; like shadows he passed through them. They screeched and buffeted him with their wings, but he walked on. They whispered horrible curses into his mind, but he walked on. The mouth of hell belched fire at him, but still he walked on.

But then came the most horrible thought of all, carried by a demon from the mouth of the wounded Apollyon: "God has abandoned you!" Christian could hardly move, his despair was so deep. "God has abandoned you!" the voice in his mind repeated. "God has abandoned you!" Christian lurched, and caught himself just before plummeting into the dark depths beside the path.

"Though I walk through the Valley of the Shadow of Death, I will fear no evil, for Thou art with me."

Christian looked up, startled. He did not know who had said these words, but he did know that someone else was in the valley. And he knew that he had not been abandoned: "Thou art with me."

"What is your name, friend?" called out Christian, but the wailing of the frustrated demons hid any answer that might have come back. Given new strength by the words he had heard, Christian walked on.

The further he walked, the thinner were the demons' voices, so that after several hours he could no longer hear them at all. Through the whole night he had been heading to the east, and now when the sun rose it seemed to spring up into the sky. It even looked larger, as though somehow he was getting closer to it. He did not see who had called out in the valley, and when he looked back the way he had come he could see only the thin, winding path and the demons still dancing around the mouth of hell. He shuddered, but when he looked ahead, he realized that he was not out of the valley yet.

Ahead of him, the path was set with traps, snares, and nets. All around it and through it were deep pits, so many that if he had had a thousand lives, he would have lost them all in trying to travel that path in the dark. But the rising sun showed every danger clearly, so that

PAGAN

Christian could leap over the pits, spring the traps, and slash through the nets.

Even so, when he got to the end of the valley, he found it a place where many who had made it even this far had been killed. It was a place of blood and bones and mangled bodies, the victims of a giant who brooded in a cave nearby, watching for pilgrims. He was named Pagan, and he might have given Christian a hard time, except that his age had made him slow and weak. He only stared at Christian, biting his nails. Christian, whose hand had gone to the hilt of his sword, relaxed. Here was no danger, and now he was out of the valley.

In my dream I saw Christian take the last few steps out of the valley. The armor that had gleamed so brilliantly at the Palace Beautiful was now as dented and stained as any that had been in the Armory. But Christian himself looked—it is hard to think of the right word—bigger. No, not just bigger, but bolder, more certain. His strides were longer, his head higher. And he seemed to look further, as though he hoped to glimpse something just over the horizon.

This is a man of intent, I thought.

And so the dream went on.

V

AS CHRISTIAN STEPPED OUT OF THE valley, he found himself on a small ascent. From it he could see all the land before him, and there, far away, he saw a man running as fast as he could away from him. Cupping his hands to his mouth, Christian called out, "So ho!" The man did not turn but seemed to run even faster.

Had this been one of the others whom Christian had met along his way, he may not have decided to go after him. But he thought that this might be someone he recognized from the City of Destruction, and he was sure that this was the one who had so encouraged him back in the valley. Christian set off at a brisk run, holding his sword against his thigh to keep it from slapping against him. Running fully armored, it was not long before his side started to pain him, but he kept on.

The man in front of him was slowing down. At first he had run out of fear of the valley, but now that he had left the valley behind him, the energy of fear was seeping away, so that soon Christian had almost reached him. Once he was closer, Christian recognized him—Faithful, his former neighbor. And Christian, perhaps to show off a bit, ran past him, holding his breathing so that it sounded regular. He

had gone only a few paces past Faithful, however, before his breath gave out, and he stumbled on a small rise. He sprawled in the dust.

"Christian?" asked Faithful.

Christian nodded sheepishly.

"Can I help you up?"

Christian held up his hand and then smiled. "Not the best introduction."

Faithful smiled as well. "With old friends, it does not matter. I have been looking for you for some time."

"For me?"

"Yes. I left Destruction soon after you. Though at first everyone laughed at your running away, soon enough the mountains above us seemed to be burning brighter, and everyone said that the town would be destroyed."

"So everyone has gone, then."

"No," said Faithful. "It is as though they did not believe what they saw. I was the only one to go out."

There was a long pause. Christian was afraid to ask his next question, and Faithful was afraid to have him ask it.

"Is my family still in town?"

"I do not know," Faithful answered. "When I left town, I walked by your house. It seemed closed up, yet there were lights in it."

Christian sighed. "It seems that I am not to hear about them for a time. But it is good to have a companion."

"Yes," agreed Faithful. "Especially after we have been through that valley." They shuddered as they remembered what they had passed through, and both were quiet for a time.

As the day passed, they talked about their journeys. They had met many of the same people, though Faithful had not met with Apollyon. (Perhaps it was while Christian was recovering from his battle that Faithful had passed him on the path.) Faithful told Christian about Wanton, who tried to lure him from the path. "She wanted to do me mischief," he said. And he had met Moses, who beat him mercilessly for disobeying his laws. And Talkative, who had deceived him for a time by talking about grace when he did not truly believe in it. And in the Valley of Humiliation, Faithful had met Shame, who had almost convinced him to turn back.

As Faithful spoke, Christian understood how many difficulties had come upon them both, and how good the Owner of that land had been to them. How many times had each of them almost turned back! And each time there had been a moment of grace to save them.

Christian put his hand on Faithful's shoulder. "And now, good friend, we go forward together!" Faithful smiled, and they walked on.

It was not long before they found themselves in a wilderness. The path was quite overgrown (it had been little used), and they were forced to walk one behind the other, Christian on ahead, slashing at the undergrowth with his sword. It was slow going, and by the time they reached the far side of the wilderness, the sun had started to go down. Both Faithful and Christian had been looking back over their shoulders; they had hoped to get much further away from the demons of the valley.

"It will not be long now," said Christian cheerfully. "We are almost out of the wilderness, and I see a town not far away where we might find rooms."

"I shall be glad to be out of this wilderness. I fear what lies behind us. Every so often I look back and it seems as if the brush parts and out steps a . . ." He stopped.

"A what?" asked Christian.

Faithful did not answer. Instead, he grabbed Christian's shoulder and turned him around. "There!" he cried, pointing fearfully back the way they had come. "Do you see it?"

Christian brought his sword in front of him. It had been a long day, and he had not slept the night before. He was already weary. If it should be Apollyon . . .

"Do you often greet old friends in this manner?" called a voice. Christian recognized it immediately. He smiled broadly and sheathed his sword.

EVANGELIST

"Evangelist," he sighed.

And so it was. Along the path Evangelist came swiftly; the underbrush did not seem to disturb him. He held his arms out, and Christian rushed to him.

"Well met," said Christian. "Well met."

"Peace be to you, dearly beloved," replied Evangelist, "and to you also," he continued, turning to Faithful.

"Welcome to our company," Faithful responded.

"As to that, we shall see how welcome the news I bring may be. But first tell me how it has been with you since our last parting." Christian and Faithful laughed. So many things had happened to them. Where should they start? "Start at the Cross," suggested Evangelist, and so they did, leaving out nothing that had occurred.

"And so at last," Christian concluded, "we have arrived at this place, our trials behind us, and that pleasant town before us on the way to the Celestial City."

Evangelist sighed deeply and, it seemed, sadly. "That town is indeed before you on the way to the Celestial City," he said, "but it is not what you suspect. You have both done well. You see the crown before you, and you have run hard for it. But the race is not over. Even if all others fall away, remember that the race is not over."

"Then neither are our trials," observed Faithful.

"No indeed," answered Evangelist, shaking his head. "The town before you is Vanity Fair. It is a place that seems pleasant at first, like a picture that looks better far away than close up. But it is a place of murder and falseness, of cruelty and deceit, a place where all manner of things are sold for profit, including men and women and children. It is a place of dreams turned to nightmares. There is no good in it."

"Then we will pass through when night falls," decided Christian.

Evangelist shook his head again. "I will not see one of you again before he reaches the Celestial City."

"What do you mean?" asked Faithful. "If we two will be together, how is it that you can see one without the other?"

"After a few days, you will no longer be together."

There was a long pause as Christian and Faithful looked at each other.

"Whatever happens once you are in that town," continued Evangelist, "remember the true Owner of this place. Remember His love. Commit yourself to Him."

Christian and Faithful walked several paces forward and stood at the edge of the wilderness, looking across the plain that divided them from Vanity Fair. "And if . . ." started Faithful, turning back to Evangelist. But he had disappeared. "He's gone!"

Christian smiled, a bit weakly. "He comes and goes as he wishes." After a pause he said, "If we are of the same mind, you were about to ask if we could go around Vanity Fair rather than through it.

But the path runs straight and true into the town." He looked up at the trees and listened deeply to all the sounds around him. Far off from them a woodpecker rattled against a dead trunk, and closer in a choir of swallows and finches and martins twittered and chirruped. But Christian was thinking of other voices, other songs.

"Do you suppose," Christian said aloud, "that Christiana has . . ." He did not finish. The birds were suddenly quiet, and several moments went by with almost no sound but a light wind turning the leaves. "Rain tonight," Christian said, and then he smiled and clapped Faithful on the shoulder. "The hard but right way," he said.

"The hard but right way," Faithful repeated. Together they went out of the wilderness and crossed the plain to Vanity Fair.

They heard what was going on long before they saw anything of the streets of that town. There was such yammering and jammering and shouting and calling and just plain noise that Faithful and Christian could hardly talk to each other. Shoulder to shoulder they walked into the town, and immediately a crowd of vendors started to call to them. (Some of them, it seemed to Christian, had voices that sounded like Apollyon's.) The goods in the stalls looked bright and new, but when Christian looked closer, he saw that the gold on the jewelry was really cheap paint, the precious stones only colored glass. The fruit was rotten, the china only clay, the charms worthless. The jugglers and clowns were really pickpockets. The vendors were selling anything they could — they would have sold their souls if they could have laid their hands upon them.

Christian and Faithful tried to pass on through, but soon such a hubbub rose around them that they became the center of the crowd. Their clothes were different from the ragged costumes of the townspeople of Vanity Fair, and they spoke much more softly and gently, so that soon even the children of Vanity Fair were laughing and pointing at them. But even so they might have escaped, except that the merchants noticed that they would not buy anything.

"What will you buy?" one called.

"See the pretty baubles," cried a woman, holding up enormous earrings against her rouged cheeks.

WHAT WILL YOU BUY?

"This document, good sir, will get you into the Celestial City itself," claimed another, holding up a torn parchment that looked something like Christian's Roll.

Finally, a burly, square merchant blocked their path, and as the townspeople encircled them, he pointed a square finger. "What will you buy?" he demanded.

"The Truth," Christian answered softly.

"We will have none of that. There is nothing in this whole world that cannot be bought in this city. Now, what will you buy?"

"The Truth," Faithful repeated.

While some laughed at the strange answers, the merchants grew angry, and soon their anger spread to others, so that Christian and Faithful found themselves facing a mob. If the burgomeister of the town had not sent his soldiers to arrest the two of them right then, the townspeople might have torn up cobblestones from the streets to fling at them. As it was, the crowd followed them to the burgomeister's house. Many squeezed inside and watched, muttering, as Christian and Faithful were examined.

The burgomeister was a fat fellow dressed in bright yellow. He oozed into a gold-plated chair and sucked the grease from his lunch off fat fingers.

"Who are you?"

"Two pilgrims on the way to the Celestial City."

"Is it your habit to cause riots wherever you go?"

"No," answered Christian.

"And yet you have chosen to do so here." At this the merchants shouted in agreement. "They would not buy any of our wares," accused one loudly.

The burgomeister leaned forward in his chair. It was not easy for him, but he was astonished. "You would not buy?" he asked.

"No."

"Nothing at all?"

"We would buy nothing but the Truth."

"What is Truth?" asked the burgomeister, but he would not stay for an answer. He turned to one of his soldiers, whispered a command, and then stood up to make his official pronouncement. "We find these two to be nothing but madmen. For their own protection and for our amusement, we judge that they should be put in a cage and kept in the town square until such time as we have judged what to do with them."

Christian's armor and sword were torn from him, and he and Faithful were set in a cage. For three days the townspeople of Vanity Fair laughed at them, spit at them, threw rotten vegetables at them, and competed to see who could be the most vile to them.

All this time, however, Christian and Faithful remained calm, quietly encouraging one another. When the people screamed at them, they sang hymns. When they demanded why the two would not buy anything, Christian and Faithful replied that the town's wares belonged to Apollyon and his kind. When the people threatened them with the burgomeister's anger, they answered that their lives were in the hands of the true Owner of that land.

Their quiet answers convinced some in Vanity Fair that Faithful and Christian were guiltless, and that they should be freed and sent on their way. "There are some of us here who trade at this fair," called one of these men, "who deserve to be in that cage more than these two!"

The merchants were not pleased with this. "Are you suggesting, sir," one answered, "that our wares are not fit to be bought?"

"Not by any honest man."

"Scoundrel!"

"Thief!"

"Liar!"

And soon there was another riot in Vanity Fair, this time right in front of the cage that held Christian and Faithful. The burgomeister's soldiers came again to bring the two prisoners in front of the burgomeister.

They had to wait some time in front of his house. It was only noon, and he had not yet risen from bed. When he did appear, his eyes were red and bleary, and he yawned heavily.

"So, my lunatic friends, you are not content with only one riot."

Christian and Faithful did not answer.

"If you will cause such mischief even from within a cage, what shall we do with you?"

No answer. The burgomeister grew angry. He still had not had his breakfast.

"If that cage will not keep you quiet, then we will see what the grave will do. To trial!" At the command, the soldiers chained the arms and legs of the two prisoners and made them shuffle along until they reached the courthouse. Before they arrived, the merchants had pushed in ahead and filled the courtroom so that those who supported Christian and Faithful could not enter. The burgomeister had come in and put on a great white wig. He had not had time to adjust it, so it slanted across his forehead. Christian and Faithful were tied to seats directly in front of him, but he would not look at them.

"My Lord Hate-Good," said the burgomeister slowly, addressing the prosecutor. "Please remember in your prosecution of this case that we have yet to dine this morning. Shall we keep these proceedings brief?"

"Yes, my lord." Hate-Good was a thin, yellowish man dressed in black. He had long, thin fingers that he clasped and unclasped in front of him, and dead eyes that looked as though they had no sight in them.

"Call your first witness."

"I call Envy."

Envy sidled up to the witness stand.

"You have known these prisoners?" asked Lord Hate-Good.

"For quite a long time, my lord. Especially this Faithful."

"And you know them to be enemies of Vanity Fair?"

"Dreadful enemies, my lord."

"How have they shown this?" Lord Hate-Good leered at the prisoners.

"My lord, since his youth Faithful has condemned the religion of our town, saying that Apollyon and his master were hateful."

At this, Lord Hate-Good shook his head. "Is there anything further?"

"I have much more I could say," replied Envy, "but I do not wish to keep the court too long. Is it not enough that as these men were being punished for causing riots in our streets, they spent their time singing idle songs?"

All the merchants nodded their agreement, and Envy stepped down.

Next Superstition was called. He was an old, old man who was so hunched over that he could only look sideways.

"Do you know these men?" asked Lord Hate-Good.

"I do not know them, my lord, nor do I wish to know such men. This Faithful is a pestilent fellow. I heard him say that our love of Apollyon and our desire to follow and please him were unnatural and evil."

"Do you deny this?" asked the burgomeister of Faithful.

"I do not deny it."

"Then you stand condemned by your own admission!"

LORD HATE-GOOD AND THE BURGOMEISTER

"My lord," said Hate-Good, bowing slightly toward the burgomeister, "I have one more witness to call before you pass sentence."

"Be quick, then."

"Yes, my lord. I call Ingratitude."

Ingratitude was a young, lusty man with thick, black curls. He held his head high in the air, perhaps to keep his nose above the cloud of perfume that adorned him. He spoke to no one less wealthy than he, and so he spoke only to the burgomeister.

"My lord, I have little to add. We have all heard these two, especially this Faithful, speak against our lord Apollyon. To this might be added the horrible arrogance of these men. I have heard the one called Faithful claim that his life was not in your lordship's hands at all. He believes you have no power over him."

The burgomeister was now so angry that he could barely speak. He looked at Faithful, and through clenched teeth he said, "So that all may know our gentleness to you, you may speak before we pass sentence."

"What can I say that will have any meaning to you? The Lord have mercy on my soul," answered Faithful.

"May he indeed have mercy, for we will have none," sneered the burgomeister. "To be proper, we shall first hear from the jury." He turned to them. "What say you of this Faithful?"

45

"I hate his looks!" cried Mr. Malice, pointing at Faithful. "Away with him!"

"Yes, away with him," agreed Mr. Live-Loose. "He will always be condemning the way I live."

Mr. Highmind called him a "sorry scrub," and Mr. Cruelty suggested that hanging would be too good for him. The foreman of the jury, Mr. Blindman, concluded that Faithful was guilty, "and we urge your lordship to deal severely with this Faithful."

At this the merchants roared, but the burgomeister silenced them with one up-raised hand. "So we shall." The burgomeister stood up. "Faithful, we condemn you to instant and immediate execution."

The soldiers rushed at Faithful, un-bound him from his chair, and pushed him out of the courthouse. The crowd fol-lowed, jeering and laughing and singing. They had forgotten Christian, still bound to his chair in the courtroom. He had not been able to say anything to Faithful over the noise of the court. He strained at the cords binding him so that he might at least get to the window that overlooked the town square. But he could only just see the sky, which had suddenly become overcast with dark clouds. The crowd out in the square grew louder, and then sud-denly it was very, very still. A minute went by, two minutes. And then the crowd roared again, louder than before.

Christian wept. And then—he could not be sure, since tears filled his eyes—it seemed that a tremendous light filled the window, and Christian thought he saw two horses and a chariot of fire wing down from the clouds toward the square. When it came up again, Faithful was in-side. He looked different; he seemed dressed in light. To the sound of glad trumpets, the horses stampeded up into the sky. The dark clouds parted, and they were gone.

Suddenly the doors to the courtroom opened, and Christian looked around. He was sure that it was the merchants return-

HOPEFUL

ing, but instead it was a youth, one of those who had tried to protect him while he was in the cage. He carried a sack be-

neath one arm, and came quickly across the courtroom, unbound Christian, and helped him up.

"Make haste," he whispered. "Though there are some of us that would help you, there are more of the merchants who wish to kill you, as they have killed your friend."

"But Faithful is not dead," replied Christian.

"I know that now," he answered. "I am Hopeful, and I want to be your companion on your journey." He handed him the sack. "Here is your armor and sword."

Christian smiled, and leaning against Hopeful (his legs were still strained from the ropes that had bound him), Christian escaped from Vanity Fair.

In my dream I saw them top a rise and leave Vanity Fair behind them. As for the people there, some were preparing to follow Christian and Hopeful away from the evil of the town. But most of the townspeople soon settled back into their old habits. When last I saw them, they had just chased a messenger out of town. He told them that Apollyon had been defeated in battle, but they would not believe him.

Hopeful could not take the place of Faithful, it seemed. As I watched the two

pilgrims, Christian would from time to time look into the sky, as if he expected to see the fiery chariot. But still, Christian knew that the Owner of the land had provided this young companion, and he was glad. And each step brought them closer to the Celestial City.

VI

THE PATH AHEAD OF THEM WAS STRAIGHT and true, and for a time Christian and Hopeful traveled along as fast as they could. The trial had taken most of the early afternoon, and after three hours of walking both pilgrims were tired. They sat down under a spreading oak tree to eat a cold supper that Hopeful had hastily put together before they had left Vanity Fair.

MR. BY-ENDS

As they were eating, a man came up the path toward them. "Well met," called the traveler.

"Well met," they replied. "Come share our supper."

"With a good will," said the man, and he too sat down. He was a well-dressed man of pleasant appearance. His smile was broad, though it never changed.

"What is your name?" asked Christian.

"I am a stranger to you both, and you to me. But if you are going along this path, I will be glad of your company. If not, then I must be content."

Hopeful leaned over and whispered to Christian, "He seems to be a fair gentleman. Shall we ask him to join us?"

"One moment," answered Christian. "I have seen many along this path who have seemed to be fair gentlemen and who later turned out to be something quite different." He turned to the stranger. "Are you from these parts?"

"No, I am from the town of Fair-Speech, and my family is old in that city. Perhaps you have heard of them: Mr. Smoothman, Mr. Facing-Both-Ways, Mr. Two-Tongues?"

"I have heard of them," answered Christian.

"Then you know our motto: 'Never strive against wind or tide.'"

"What does that mean?" asked Hopeful.

"It means, my young friend, that we should always try to get along, that we should never disagree with others."

"But suppose," asked Hopeful, "that the others are wrong?"

"It would be good to bear in mind that there are always two sides to every question. Perhaps no one is ever completely wrong."

"Now I do know you," said Christian. "You are Mr. By-Ends, who never holds any opinion or any belief that is not acceptable to anyone else."

"It is not a name I like, but one given to me by malicious persons."

"But it is a name that fits!"

"If you wish," Mr. By-Ends replied.

"If you are to be our companion on this path, you must go against wind and tide . . ."

"But . . ."

". . . and take the hard but right way to come to the Celestial City."

Mr. By-Ends stood up and stepped back from them. "I see that if I were to go with you, you would not allow me my liberty. So, with your leave, I shall wait for more agreeable companions." With that, he left them and sat down by the side of the path.

Christian and Hopeful finished their supper and headed down the path. There were still some three hours of daylight left, and they hoped to walk four or five miles further. When they reached a turn in the path, they looked back to see whether Mr. By-Ends had followed, but they saw instead that he was talking with three new companions. Hopeful recognized them. They were from Vanity Fair, and their names were Mr. Moneylove, Mr. Lovegain, and Mr. Coveting. As Christian and Hopeful watched, they each bowed to one another and clapped each other on the shoulders. Mr. By-Ends pointed up the path at Christian and Hopeful and said something to his new friends. They all began laughing, and then turned and walked down the path. Christian and Hopeful went on, trying to keep their distance, though it seemed as if the others were trying to catch up.

But Christian and Hopeful were themselves moving quickly. They crossed a narrow plain called Ease, and as the light began to fade, they arrived at a small hill. At the bottom of the hill stood a crooked old man named Lucre.

"Today is a lucky day for you," he called cheerfully. "I have just discovered a silver mine in that hill, and if you will come with me now, for only a little digging you will soon be wealthy beyond your imaginings."

"Let us go see," said Hopeful, taking a step off the path.

"No," said Christian, pulling him back. "Nothing must turn us from the path."

"Beyond belief," repeated Lucre.

LUCRE

Christian looked up at the top of the hill and the opening of the mine. "That looks like a dangerous place."

"No, no," answered Lucre, "only to those who are careless."

"Then we shall not be careless," said Christian, and he and Hopeful walked on. They did not know, though they might have guessed, that Mr. By-Ends and his companions did not hesitate to leave the path. They climbed up to the mine's opening and peered in. But the ground beneath them gave way, and they tumbled down into the mine. No one ever saw them again.

Christian and Hopeful were cheerful as they walked on, and perhaps rather proud of having held off against Lucre's temptation. But if they were proud, they were brought up short by a statue carved in white stone. It was of a woman, looking back over her shoulder.

"The writing on it is worn. Can you read it?" asked Hopeful.

Christian nodded. " 'Remember Lot's wife.' " He paused, and then said thoughtfully, "She too escaped one temptation, only to be destroyed by the next."

"Perhaps," said Hopeful, "this statue is meant to be a sign from the Owner."

"If so, it is a fearsome sign," replied Christian. "We must be on our guard."

As they went on their way, they came to a river whose waters sparkled gold in the setting sun. They knelt, gathered water in their cupped hands, and then drank deeply. Because the river flowed out of Emmanuel's land, a single draft from it filled them and livened their spirits. Green fruit trees grew on the banks of the river, bearing peaches and pears larger than any that had grown in the valley of the City of Destruction. Christian and Hopeful ate of the fruit, and then sat down in a meadow filled with lilies so white it almost hurt their eyes to look at them. The lily scent lay on the breeze, and as the sun set, the flowers turned golden.

Christian and Hopeful lay down and went to sleep. Since Christian had left the Palace Beautiful, this was the first place that he was able to lie down in safety and comfort. When the two pilgrims woke, they ate from the fruit of the trees and drank from the river and slept again. And so it went for three days and three nights. At the end of that time they were refreshed, strong, and eager to push on to the journey's end.

But in those three days they had forgotten the statue of Lot's wife.

On the morning of the fourth day, they set out again on the path. For a time the river ran beside it, and as the path grew dusty they would stop and refresh themselves. But just before noon, they reached a point where the path parted from the river. It grew rough and dry and filled with sharp stones. Thinking of the beautiful meadow they had left behind, Christian and Hopeful became discouraged. The high stone wall that ran beside the path reflected back the heat of a scorching sun, and soon the two grew weak and faint.

They were almost spent when the wall stopped abruptly, and Christian and Hopeful saw a beautiful fenced meadow spread out before them. It seemed like the one they had left behind, and they stepped to the fence eagerly. There were no lilies here, and in fact all the flowers that were open in the meadow seemed not quite the right color. The red roses were so red as to seem almost black, and the yellow ones looked garish and hard. But Christian did not notice.

"It looks like the meadow runs along the path," he said excitedly. "Let's cross into it. It will be easier walking."

Hopeful was wary. "But suppose the meadow leads us away from the path?"

"The path will wind around. We'll meet it on the far side." And without waiting for Hopeful to answer, Christian jumped over the fence and set out. Hopeful followed, a bit slowly.

It was true that the walking was much easier in the meadow, and Hopeful's fears were quieted when they met another traveler, Mr. Vain-Confidence.

"Where are you headed?" Christian asked.

"To the gates of the Celestial City," he answered.

Christian looked back at Hopeful. "You see?" he said.

They walked on, and as night began to fall they searched for a place to sleep. But the ground around them had suddenly grown soggy, and though the trees back by the path had been blossoming, the ones here were dead or covered with poisonous vines.

In the growing darkness Mr. Vain-Confidence had not slowed his pace, and he was now a short distance ahead of them. But when they called out, there was no answer from him.

"He might be further ahead than we thought," said Christian, but neither of them believed that.

"We should stop," said Hopeful.

Christian agreed, for it was now almost completely dark. "Who would have thought that this meadow should have led us out of the right way?"

Hopeful did not answer. They both knew that they should not have left the path.

They walked on for a time, until they suddenly recognized a blasted tree and realized that they had come in a circle.

"I am sorry that I have brought you out of the way," said Christian finally.

"Be comforted," said Hopeful. "I am sure that in the end, this too will be for our benefit."

As if to mock him, the skies opened up, and it began to rain and thunder. The ground, already soggy, soon became flooded, and the darkness was so deep that they could not hope to find the way back to the path. So they blundered around in the meadow, hoping that the lightning might reveal some shelter. It never did, and so they huddled at the foot of an oak tree and waited for the dawn. When it came, the rain stopped, but by then the two were so weary that they fell asleep.

It was a mistake. If they had tried to get back to the path when dawn first showed, they might have made it. It would have been a near thing, but they might have made it. But instead they slept and did not hear the rumbling footsteps of the giant who saw them, crouched over them, and grabbed each of them by the neck.

"Who are you?" he demanded in a grim voice.

"Two pilgrims on the way to the Celestial City," replied Christian, trembling. "We have lost our way."

The giant laughed maliciously. "So you have," he answered. "You have trespassed and trampled on my ground, the grounds of Giant Despair. Now you pay the price of your error." So saying, he pushed them ahead of him to Doubting Castle, his home.

It was a tall, dark place, with grim

battlements and walls so thick that twenty men could stand shoulder to shoulder

and not span them. No flags flew from the turrets; no banners hung from the walls.

And there was not a single window in the entire castle.

Giant Despair dragged Hopeful and Christian down, down, down into the bowels of the castle and threw them into a dungeon, locking the iron door after them. He hurled Christian's armor and sword against the wall outside. "Much good may they do you here," he laughed.

There was no light in the dungeon, so they could not see the size of the room they were in. But they knew it was a grim place. They could hear scurrying creatures around them, and eyes that glowed with a light of their own peered evilly out of the blackness. They leaned against clammy walls, afraid to sit down. They held their breath as much as they could, the air stank so awfully.

Hopeful tried to get Christian to sing a hymn, but Christian could not. It was because of him that they had come to this, and he could not forgive himself. He did not think that he could ever be forgiven, or that they would ever find their way back to the path.

They could not tell how much time passed while they were in the dungeon. But with no food and no water but the sweat of the rock walls, they grew weaker and weaker. And Christian would not be comforted.

After a long time, the giant's wife, named Giantess Diffidence, asked her husband whether they were still alive.

"I suppose so," answered Giant Despair.

"Don't you think you should go and see?"

"And suppose they are?" He was busy eating an ox, and he did not want to trudge all the way down to the dungeon just to see if Christian and Hopeful were still breathing.

"Then beat them until they wish to do away with themselves."

Giant Despair sighed, pushed away from the table, and went down to the dungeon. When he opened the door and shoved in a torch, Christian and Hopeful had to shield their eyes against the sudden light.

"Have you come to let us out?" asked Hopeful. The giant laughed and held up a great cudgel made from the trunk of a crab-apple tree. He swung it against Hopeful's chest, knocking him back into the mud of the dungeon. When Christian bent over him, the giant swung his club against Christian's side, knocking him against one of the walls. Giant Despair continued swinging his club until the two were both unconscious.

For three more days, Giant Despair came to the dungeon each morning. On the third day, Christian ducked under one of the giant's blows and the club struck the wall, dislodging a stone. A tiny shaft of sunlight eked its way in, striking the giant in the forehead. Instantly all his strength

left him, and he had to crawl out of the dungeon and fumble at the door before he could lock it. Had Christian and Hopeful been stronger and not so weakened by their time in the dungeon, they might have escaped.

That night, Giantess Diffidence visited them for the first time.

"You are stout men to be still alive," she said. "But you must realize that you will not escape. Every morning my husband will beat you. Every evening you will fall asleep without having eaten. This kind of bitter life is not worth living."

Christian nodded his head and sank to the ground.

"You must be hungry now," she said. She set down a burlap bag just inside the door. "What is in here will relieve you." She clanged the door shut, and they heard her slow steps ascending the stairs.

Hopeful rushed to the bag and opened it, holding it to the shaft of light. "This is strange," he said. "Here is a rope, a knife, and a bottle."

"She wants us to kill ourselves," replied Christian. "The rope will hang us, the knife will stab us, and whatever is in the bottle will surely poison us." He paused for a moment and then said slowly, "Perhaps it would be best."

"No!" cried Hopeful, horrified. "We cannot let Despair lead us to self-murder! Did you not see how the giant was weakened by the light? Who knows but that we might have escaped if we had been prepared. Let us be patient and wait for our opportunity."

And so they waited. Each day the giant came and beat them, and each night they fell asleep without having eaten. Christian eyed the burlap bag, but he took nothing from it.

Finally Giantess Diffidence grew impatient. One night, as she lay in bed with her husband, she hit upon a plan.

"Tomorrow morning, before you beat them, take them into the castle yard and show them the bones and skulls of those you have already killed. Make them believe that before another week has passed, you will tear them in pieces and leave their bones on top of this pile."

In the morning, this is just what the giant did.

"These bones," he told Christian and Hopeful, gesturing to the grim pile, "were once pilgrims such as you. They trespassed on my grounds, as you have done. They lay in my dungeon, as you have done. And in one week, your bones will top theirs."

Then he brought the two back to the dungeon, beat them again, and left them moaning. "They will have killed themselves by nightfall," he thought gleefully.

And indeed, the first thing that Christian did when he could move after the beating was to pick up the burlap bag.

"No!" cried Hopeful, beginning to crawl over to Christian, who had already taken out the poison. "The giant has beaten and starved me as well as you. And I too miss the light. But let us be patient a little longer."

"I cannot," said Christian, in despair.

By this time Hopeful had reached Christian. "Remember your courage in Vanity Fair. Remember your battle with Apollyon, how when you thought all was lost, your hand found your sword, as Emmanuel would have it."

Christian nodded, and then with sudden strength he threw the bottle of poison, shattering it against a wall. "As Emmanuel would have it," he said, and there was a new power in his voice.

"Let us read in our Rolls," suggested Hopeful, and they pulled them from

GIANT DESPAIR

beneath their shirts and together stood by the tiny sliver of sunlight to read.

Around noon, Giantess Diffidence heard a sound she had not heard in that castle before: the sound of singing. She listened carefully. She had not heard the

GIANTESS DIFFIDENCE

songs before, but she knew what they were. Christian and Hopeful were singing hymns.

"Hymns!" shouted Giant Despair, when she told him. "Hymns!"

"They must have some reason to hope," said the giantess thoughtfully.

"What can they hope for? They cannot escape."

"But perhaps . . . Have you searched them?"

"No."

"If they hope to escape, they may have some sort of picklocks."

The giant nodded. "If it were true, then that would give them hope. Let us divide this ox, and then I will search them."

If Giant Despair had known what Christian had found, he would not have eaten his ox first. While reading his Roll, Christian had noticed the light glinting off something buried beneath the wax

seal. With his thumbnail he scratched away the wax. Beneath it was a key, and on its shaft was one word: "Promise."

"Could it work?" asked Christian, looking toward the iron door of the dungeon.

"Try it," suggested Hopeful.

So he did. At first the lock did not turn, and Christian was ready to throw the key into the darkness.

"Trust Emmanuel," said Hopeful. "He would not put the key there if it had no purpose. Try again."

So Christian tried it again, and this time the lock turned easily. Outside the door, Christian struggled with his sword and armor, left there in a heap by the giant. Then he and Hopeful crawled up the stairs and, with the same key, opened

58

the door into the castle yard. Slowly, so slowly, they crossed the yard, knowing that they could not escape if the giant saw them. They were too weak to run.

They came to the final gate, a heavy iron one. Christian tried the key, but the lock was so rusty and the gate so heavy that he and Hopeful could not open it without a dreadful creaking.

The sound carried, and Giant Despair heard it. He put down the ox shank he was devouring and bounded into the castle yard, grabbing his club as he went. Christian and Hopeful heard the rumble of his steps, and desperately they pushed at the gate. But it opened so slowly. And then the giant was almost upon them.

He said nothing but walked to them slowly, his cudgel raised. This would be the last beating he would give them, and then he would watch their bones whiten under the skies.

Christian and Hopeful tugged at the gate. It was almost opened wide enough for them to slip through.

But now the giant stood over them. He started to swing his club, but even as he brought it from behind his back, a beam of bright sunlight pierced through the clouds that always hung above Doubting Castle, striking the giant where his heart should have been. With a terrible cry he dropped his club and fell to the ground.

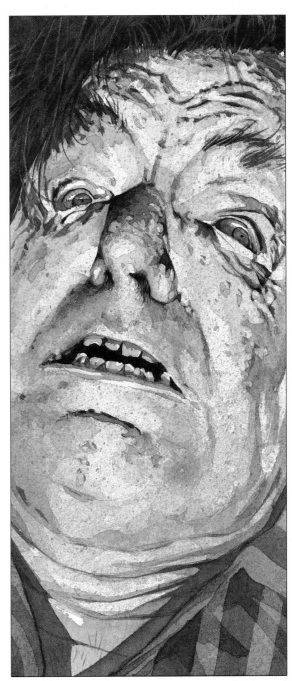

Christian and Hopeful did not wait to see if he were still alive. They struggled back to the meadow, crossed it, and climbed back over the fence to the path. They sat down, panting, weeping with joy, and laughing, all at the same time.

"You were right to hope," Christian said.

"The Owner of this land is always to be trusted," replied Hopeful.

Before they left that place, they set up a sign on the path with this warning:

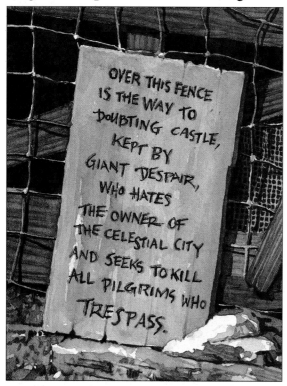

OVER THIS FENCE IS THE WAY TO DOUBTING CASTLE, KEPT BY GIANT DESPAIR, WHO HATES THE OWNER OF THE CELESTIAL CITY AND SEEKS TO KILL ALL PILGRIMS WHO TRESPASS.

For years afterward, many who followed along the path and who were tempted to cross into the meadow were saved by this sign.

In my dream I knew that Giant Despair had not died but still lived in Doubting Castle. And I also knew that not all who escaped from his castle were so hopeful. (I remembered the man in the cage at the Interpreter's House.) But Christian, together with Hopeful, was back on the path.

I wondered how much longer it would take them to reach the Celestial City. And I wondered about my own journey.

VII

AND NOW THE WAY BECAME PLEASANT, AS Christian and Hopeful neared the Delectable Mountains that Christian had seen from the high turret of the Palace Beautiful. Gardens and orchards bloomed along the path, and the air was always warm and fresh. The breeze carried along the scent of sweet apples, so that even the water tasted of it. There were fountains and clear streams, their water so cold it was startling when they first touched it, but so satisfying it made their skin tingle.

The further the two got from Doubting Castle, the more beautiful the gardens and orchards became, and the more sparkling the waters. They ate the fruit and bathed in the waters each morning, feeling themselves growing stronger, until soon it seemed that they might run all day without growing tired. They hardly noticed that the path was going higher and higher with each turning, until one morning they looked back and saw, in the hazy distance, the grey clouds that covered Doubting Castle far behind and below them. Ahead the sky seemed so blue and so close that they felt they could almost touch its glass dome.

They started out, the sun rising just in front of them. It was bigger than ever before, but the water and fruit of that land

KNOWLEDGE

had made their eyes stronger, so that they could almost look at it without blinking.

"The Celestial City must not be far from here," suggested Hopeful.

Ahead of them four shepherds were feeding their flocks alongside the pathway, and Christian wondered if they might not know how far the pilgrims still had to travel to the Celestial City. The shepherds were big, sturdy men, dressed in simple cloaks. Their eyes were a bright, bright blue, as though they had taken in the sky after all their years on the mountains. Leaning on their crooks,

the shepherds watched Christian and Hopeful approach.

"Do these mountains belong to the Owner too?" asked Christian, a bit shyly. The shepherds seemed so peaceful, so certain of what they were doing, that Christian was reluctant to disturb them.

"These mountains are Emmanuel's land, and they are within sight of His City," answered the oldest, named Knowledge. "These are His sheep, and He laid down His life for them."

"Is this the way, then, to the Celestial City?"

Knowledge leaned down and stroked the head of a sheep that had come up, bleating to be petted. "You have known all along that this is the way."

At this, a sudden hope rose strong in Christian's heart.

"How far is the Celestial City from here?"

"Too far for some, but not far for those who get there."

"And is the way safe or dangerous?"

"Safe for those for whom it is to be safe, dangerous for those for whom it is to be dangerous."

One of the other shepherds, named Sincere, saw that Christian and Hopeful were confused by these answers. "You have both known many dangers, as well as many times of safety on your journey," he explained. "You have seen the Valley of the Shadow of Death and the Palace Beautiful. You have seen Doubting Castle (yes, I can see that you have been there), and now you have come to the Delectable Mountains. Why should you be surprised to find that the way ahead of you is no different?"

Christian nodded his head. "We should not be surprised, for we are on the hard but right way."

Sincere nodded. "It is so. But that you may understand further, follow my cousins, Experience and Watchful, and they will show you what Knowledge means."

Experience and Watchful handed their crooks to Christian and Hopeful, and all four began to ascend higher into the Delectable Mountains. At each step they found a new marvel: a stream gushing from between the roots of an oak tree, two raccoons frolicking high in the branches of a maple, a carpet of moss so soft and so thick that they felt that they walked on downy feathers.

When they reached the top, the shepherds told Christian and Hopeful to look down. They stood on a sheer cliff, and they were so high up that Christian and Hopeful did not want to get close to the drop-off. When they did peer over, having crawled to the edge on their hands and knees, they saw, far below them, the bones of those who had fallen. Black, wispy smoke hovered over the remains.

This is the Cliff of Error," said Watchful. "Some of the bones below were put there by Giant Despair, but most are from those who blinded themselves with fear and uncertainty and left the path. They stumbled here and fell to the bottom."

"Where is the smoke from?" asked Hopeful.

"It runs through a cave that ends at the bottom of the cliff and begins at the mouth of hell." Christian and Hopeful shuddered. But for the key called "Promise," Giant Despair might have added their bones to that pile.

"This is not all that we have to show you!" said Experience heartily. "Come."

They mounted to another hill, making their way along a path so steep that Christian and Hopeful had to depend on their crooks to get themselves up. At the top, Experience pointed directly east, a smile spreading across his face.

"Behold, the gates of the Celestial City."

Christian looked, but some of the smoke from the Cliff of Error had fogged his sight, and all he could see was a great light.

But Hopeful could see clearly. He held his breath. "Christian," he gasped. "They are so beautiful. And so close."

Christian looked for a long time, but he could see no more clearly than he had at first. He turned away, a little sadly. They

clambered back down the path, Experience and Watchful leading the way, and found Knowledge and Sincere gathering the sheep.

"It is late," said Knowledge. "Lodge with us this night and leave in the morning."

"Gladly," replied Christian, and so he and Hopeful stayed, sleeping peacefully with the shepherds under the bright, bright stars.

In the morning they feasted on nuts and brown bread and sweet, juicy fruits that Christian and Hopeful had never seen before. "Many things grow close to the Celestial City that can grow nowhere else," Sincere explained.

"It is another of the many wonders of this place," said Hopeful. The shepherds merely nodded.

When it was time for Christian and Hopeful to be on their way, Experience gave two warnings. "First, beware of the Deceiver," he said. "He will seem fair to you, but you will know in your hearts that he is evil. Second, do not fall asleep on the Enchanted Ground. You will know why when you come to it. Godspeed on your journey."

By now all the sheep were bleating for their pastures, so the shepherds, waving farewell, took their animals up into the mountains. Christian and Hopeful watched them until they were out of sight, and then they turned to the path. They walked briskly for most of the morning; the path was easy as they were coming down off the mountains. Hopeful was still full of his sight of the gates to the Celestial City, and though Christian wished that he too had seen them, he was cheered by Hopeful's vision.

At the foot of the mountains, a small, crooked lane came into the path, a short-cut from a country called Conceit. A young fellow was just skipping off that lane into the path, and his name was Ignorance. Just that morning he had decided to try the path. He had had nothing else to do.

"Well met," he called cheerfully. "Are you also headed toward the Celestial City?"

"Yes," answered Christian. "We are. But we came in at the Shining Gate and have followed the path. Will you have some trouble getting into the Celestial City without having traveled the path from its beginnings?"

At this Ignorance looked annoyed. "I know the Owner of these lands. I have lived well, and have left my country to follow the path."

"But you have not received a Roll."

"Gentlemen, you are both strangers to me. Be content to follow your own religion, and leave me to follow mine."

Hopeful looked at him questioningly. "But don't you want to know how to travel the path?"

Ignorance shook his head and pointed to the ground. "A path is a path."

"But this one begins at the Shining Gate."

Again Ignorance shook his head. "As everyone in my country knows, the Shining Gate you speak of is far away. No one in my country even knows the way to it, nor do they need to, since we have such a fine, pleasant green lane that comes down from Conceit into the path. So let us all hope for the best when we reach the Celestial City!"

Christian shook his head. "He does not seem to want to know how to follow the hard but right way," he whispered to Hopeful.

"I have known many like him in Vanity Fair."

"And I in the City of Destruction," answered Christian. They walked on ahead, Ignorance following some ways behind, unwilling to talk further.

Around noon they began to smell smoke, and soon they saw black billows of it rising above the trees in front of them. It seemed as if the woods themselves must be on fire, but the smoke was more dreadful. Christian suddenly remembered where he had smelled it before.

"Hopeful," he said, "that is the smell of . . ."

He did not finish, for immediately before them a band of demons was cavorting on the path and coming toward them, singing and dancing. Christian and Hopeful stepped to the side, Christian holding his shield before both of them. As the demons passed, Christian looked into the middle of the company. There he thought he saw someone he knew, a man named Turn-Away, who at one time had left the City of Destruction. But Christian could not be sure, since the man hung his head and kept his face to the ground. The smell of the demons and their heat made it impossible for Christian to look long.

None of the demons had stopped or spoken to Christian and Hopeful as they passed, but as the two men watched them head back away from the Celestial City, they saw them stop by Ignorance, who cowered on the edge of the path. The demons leered into his face and pinched his skin as though testing it for freshness.

IGNORANCE

Christian and Hopeful saw them hold out their hands. Perhaps they were asking to see his Roll. But when he could not show it, the demons laughed, threw ropes around Ignorance, jerked him into their midst, and danced away, back toward the Cliff of Error. Christian and Hopeful shuddered.

They turned back to the path. Much of the grass on it had been burned by the demons' feet, and some of the roots that ran across it had been torn up by their clawed heels. But as the two went further, they saw that the path seemed to be healing, the grass growing where it had been burned, and the roots easing themselves back into the rich earth. Soon even the acrid smell of the demons was gone, blown away in the light breezes that came down off the Delectable Mountains.

In the late afternoon, Christian and Hopeful, now a little tired from their journey, came to a place where another path joined their path. In fact, both ways seemed to go straight ahead, and neither pilgrim could decide which way to take. Both seemed fair, and both seemed to head toward the Celestial City.

"Which way?" asked Hopeful.

Christian shook his head. "I do not know."

"Gentlemen, perhaps I may be of some service." The smooth voice came from a tall figure covered entirely by a hooded white cloak. They did not know how they could have missed seeing him standing there before.

"Do you know the way to the Celestial City?" Christian asked.

The figure nodded slowly. They could not see his face, since it was shrouded by the white hood. "I wait here for pilgrims such as you, who are on their way to the Celestial City. Many have followed me before, and now I offer my small services to you. Would you too care to follow me?"

Christian turned to Hopeful, speaking quietly. "I do not like this fellow. He is too . . . hidden."

Hopeful agreed. "And yet, he is dressed all in white. Perhaps he is one of the Shining Ones who live in the Celestial City, sent here to be a guide for pilgrims."

"Perhaps." Christian thought for a moment, then decided. "Let us follow him." Christian turned to the figure. "Lead on," he said.

So the white figure took the left fork, and almost immediately the path began to lead away from the Celestial City. Christian and Hopeful should have turned back, but the figure moved on ahead, and they followed. The path kept bending around, until finally they realized that they now had their backs to the Celestial City and were going away from it.

"Hold!" cried Christian. "This cannot be the right way."

The figure stopped and turned toward them. Slowly it raised its perfectly white hands to its hood and lowered it. They saw its face for the first time: It was a grinning skull.

"The Deceiver," whispered Christian.

They stepped back, but it was too late. A weighted net fell upon them, and as

DECEIVER

they struggled they became so entangled that they knew they could never loose themselves. The Deceiver said nothing. He put his hood back up, walked past them without looking, and headed back the way they had come so that he would be ready for any other pilgrims that came his way.

The net only grew tighter as Christian and Hopeful hung in it. Christian's hand was pinned against his side, so he could not hope to reach his sword. They had had no food or water for most of the day, and so they felt weak, and Christian began to wonder if they would ever get away. After a time, they stopped struggling.

When darkness fell, the two began to fear the animals that prowled at night. But even more they feared the Deceiver, who would have them at his mercy if he returned. And in fact, not long after it grew dark they saw a white light moving through the trees. It shone so brightly that the light seemed to push up into the sky like a beacon.

"Is that the Deceiver?" Christian whispered to Hopeful.

"No," replied Hopeful, "it cannot be. The light is so different. It is white, but it seems to be many other colors as well."

As it came closer, Christian also grew sure that it was not the Deceiver. And when it was very close and Christian saw the golden features of the One who had come to them, and felt the light that shone so full and real and warm around him, he could not understand how he and Hopeful could ever have mistaken the Deceiver for one of the Shining Ones of the Celestial City.

"What are you doing here?" asked the Shining One. "This is not the path to the Celestial City."

"No," answered Christian. "We allowed ourselves to be led out of the way by the Deceiver, and now we are caught in his net."

The Shining One took out his flaming sword and slashed the net, but left Christian and Hopeful unharmed. When the two pilgrims stood up and rubbed their strained limbs, the Shining One looked at them sternly.

"Where did you stay last night?"

"In the Delectable Mountains."

"And did the shepherds of those mountains tell you to be on your guard against the Deceiver?"

Christian and Hopeful both nodded in shame.

"Can you guess, then, where this path will lead?"

Suddenly Christian knew. "Back to the Cliff of Error."

The Shining One nodded. "If I had not come, the Deceiver would have returned later this night and dragged you to the cliff. Now follow me, and I will set you back on the right path."

So Christian and Hopeful followed. It was deep night now, so they could not have seen the path without the Shining One, whose light spread around them, twinkling on bright stones and pushing back the darkness of the woods. In a short time they had arrived back at the fork in the path. The Deceiver was nowhere in sight, though both Christian and Hopeful felt that if the Shining One were not there, the Deceiver would be.

The Shining One took them more than a mile down the right path, and then stopped. How could they thank him? And then Hopeful knew. He began to sing.

Praise God
from Whom all blessings flow.

And then Christian joined in, their voices twining and becoming as one.

Praise Him
all creatures here below.

And then the Shining One joined in with great bass tones, supporting and lifting the voices of Christian and Hopeful.

Praise Him
above ye heavenly host.
Praise Father, Son, and Holy Ghost.

The woods were quiet as the notes of the song died away. The Shining One kissed each of them on the forehead in blessing, and then left them. Christian and Hopeful lay down to sleep.

They were awakened in the morning by the quick footsteps of an old man, dressed in a professor's gown and muttering to himself. When he saw them, he stopped.

"Good morn. And where are you bound?"

"We go to the Celestial City, Hopeful and I," replied Christian. "But you, good sir, you have your back to the City."

At this the man broke into loud laughter, so horrible that it frightened the pilgrims. "My back to the City! My back to the City! And how would you know this?"

"Because," answered Christian, "this path leads to that City, and you are walking away from it."

Again the man laughed, even more horribly. He was a curious old fellow, whose eyes darted about from thing to thing, though he never looked long at any one thing, nor did he ever look at Christian and Hopeful.

"Why do you laugh?" asked Christian.

"I laugh to see what fools you are, to take such a long and hard journey for no reason at all. You have nothing but your travel for all your pains."

"Do you think we will not be received at the City?"

"Received! Received! Why man, there is no such place as you dream of in all the world!"

Christian looked stunned. Was this why he had not been able to see the gates from the Delectable Mountains? But then Hopeful answered, "We have both heard and believe that there is such a place to be found."

"When I was at home in my own country," replied the man, "I heard as you have heard. So I, like you, went out in search of this place. I have been wandering this wilderness now for forty years, and I have found no more of that city than I found on the first day I set out."

"Then you no longer believe?"

At this the man pulled out a sheaf of old maps, and with a yellowed finger he showed them all the countries he had explored. But on all those maps there was no sign of the path.

"I believed once," he said. "But I have been looking further and longer than both of you, and now I know I was a fool to believe. I am going back to the city I left behind."

ATHEIST

"Is it possible," asked Christian, "that you are Professor Atheist, who left the City of Destruction in my father's time to find the location of paradise?"

"So I am," he said, "and now I know it is not to be found." So saying, he passed Christian and Hopeful and hurried back down the path, throwing his maps aside.

Christian thought for a long time. "Could it be true?" he said quietly. "Could the Celestial City really be only a dream?"

"Not a dream," said Hopeful. "You have seen the evidence all along the path. And I have seen the gates of the City.

Look! The sun is up, and it is larger and bigger 'round than ever before. Come. Let us follow the path to the east and find the Celestial City."

Christian rose, but he walked very slowly. His gloom infected Hopeful, so that both grew weary after only a short time. The air grew heavy around them, the path was hard and tiring, and soon both pilgrims felt their eyelids grow heavy with a deep drowsiness.

"I can scarcely hold up my eyes," yawned Hopeful. "Let us lie down here and rest before we continue on our way."

Christian was about to agree.

"I wonder what place this is," mused Hopeful.

Then suddenly Christian was wide awake. Perhaps he had remembered his error at the meadow that led to Doubting Castle, or at the fork in the path. But he was not going to forget the warning of the shepherds again.

"We are on the Enchanted Ground!" he cried. "If we sleep here, we will never wake."

Hopeful rubbed his eyes; he had already fallen to one knee. Christian jerked him up and yanked him forward. "Come along!" he cried. "For the love of Emmanuel, come along!" And half-pulling Hopeful, Christian escaped from the Enchanted Ground. And Christian escaped from something else: He left behind all the doubt that Atheist had planted in him.

With new energy he and Hopeful hurried on to the Celestial City.

Past the Enchanted Ground, the Country of Beulah lay. In this land the air was sweet and pleasant, warmer even than that of the Delectable Mountains, so that the fruits that grew there were more exotic: pomegranates, apricots, and all kinds of melons. The grasses were green and long and lush, the trees flowered, and the streams as clear as those in the Delectable Mountains, only deeper and somehow merrier. Every day Christian and Hopeful discovered new flowers of delicate petals, and they heard the singing of birds in a great chorus of praise. They were so close to the sun now that it no longer set, for they were far from the Valley of the Shadow of Death, and Doubting Castle seemed only a distant memory. They knew that they were close to the Celestial City as well, for they began to see Shining Ones walking in the woods, mending the wing of a sparrow, or planting a sapling, or tending a vineyard. Christian and Hopeful were on the borders of the Celestial City.

After seven days in this country, they came to a long valley where they passed many who waved to them gladly and shouted encouragement. Christian had now completely forgotten Atheist, and he and Hopeful ran almost the length of the valley, for they knew the City had to be close.

And when they came to the valley's end and it opened out before them, there was the City indeed. They saw it rising far above them, rising into the sun, so that they suddenly knew that the light which had shone on them throughout their journey had come from the City itself. Its walls were built of pearls and precious stones, and the streets that rose higher and higher, higher than even Christian could look, were plated with gold that shone with the reflected light from the center of the City, a light that was too bright to look on, even with their strengthened eyes. If they had thought at that moment to look at themselves (they did not), they would have seen that they too were cloaked in that reflected light.

They hurried from that valley, passing orchards and vineyards and gardens whose gates opened onto the path.

"Whose good gardens are these?" Christian and Hopeful asked of the gardeners tending them.

"They are the Owner's," the gardeners replied, "planted for His own delight and the pleasure of His pilgrims." Christian and Hopeful asked to taste the fruit of one of the vineyards, and found it so sweet and so light that they felt completely refreshed after eating a single grape.

And so, with singing and great joy, they came to the end of the path, and found what they had least expected.

There seemed to be no way to reach the gates.

The path ended abruptly in a deep and dark river that flowed swiftly. Hopeful and Christian could see no bottom. They looked up and down each bank. They could see no bridge.

Across the river, two Shining Ones appeared, one sitting on a large, round stone marked with a broken seal, set before an opened cave.

"Is there no way across?" Christian called out to them.

"There is no bridge," the Shining Ones answered.

"Is there no other way?"

"None for you. You must go through the waters or you cannot come to the gates."

Christian and Hopeful walked down to the water that swirled against the banks.

"Is it deep?" Christian called to the Shining Ones.

They shrugged. "You shall find it deep or shallow, depending on how firmly you believe in the Owner of this place." Then the two Shining Ones vanished.

A look of determination filled Christian's face as he and Hopeful stepped into the waters. At first he kept his eyes on the gates of the Celestial City, and the bottom of the river seemed firm. His feet were hardly wet. But then he looked down to the water, and suddenly he remembered

Apollyon's charge that he had been disloyal to Emmanuel. And he remembered all the times that he had left the path. Then the river seemed to rise up against him in foaming waves, and he felt the bottom slip away. Desperately he looked up

to the City, but a mist had come up from the river and hid it from him.

"This is the River of Death," he cried, and then fell under the waters, into darkness and horror.

Hopeful struggled to pull Christian's head above the water.

"I shall not see the land of the Celestial City," Christian sputtered.

"Do not despair!" cried Hopeful. "I see the gates already, and the Shining Ones standing on the shore to receive us." He pulled Christian through the waters.

"It is only for you that they wait," insisted Christian. "You have been hopeful since I have known you."

"And you as well. Be of good cheer. Remember: 'When I pass through the waters, Thou art with me.'"

"Thou art with me," repeated Christian. "Thou art with me." And as he remembered the Owner's promise, the waters stilled, the river bottom came back under his feet, the mist cleared, and Christian saw the gates of the Celestial City again. Together Christian and Hopeful waded across the rest of the river and reached the shore of the other side.

When they came out of the waters, they felt that their bodies had changed. They were light and new and strong. All that was mortal had been washed away in the river. And Christian's armor had floated back to the other shore, where it was being reverently gathered by fair hands so that it might be carried to the Armory of the Palace Beautiful, where at this moment a new banner was being hung, with a story as new and as old as all the world.

But Christian was not thinking of this. Instead, he and Hopeful and the two Shining Ones who had again appeared were running up the steep ascent to the Celestial City. And though its foundation was above the clouds, they ran with ease, and did not grow weary.

When they arrived at the gates, the

Shining Ones said to them, "Here you will see Emmanuel as He is." The gates—they looked like the Shining Gate, but higher and brighter—opened, and the heavenly host crowded out to meet them, singing songs. And there, waving a palm and singing louder than all the rest, came Faithful.

The host gathered around them as trumpeters made heaven echo with their glad notes. The bells of the City began to ring, and when Christian and Hopeful reached the gates and held out their Rolls, a cry went up so loud and so joyous that it woke Despair back in the Interpreter's House. He looked up and, with shaking hand, reached for the door of his cage.

So Christian and Hopeful entered the Celestial City, and as they walked in they were changed in the twinkling of an eye. There were crowns on their heads, bright robes on their backs, and new words on their lips.

Holy, Holy, Holy is the Lord.
Holy is the Lord.

Christian stepped onto the gold streets, but before the gates closed, he looked back through them. He could see the whole landscape of his journey clearly, back through the Delectable Mountains to the Valley of the Shadow of Death, the Palace Beautiful, the Shining Gate, the City of Destruction, and even his own house, where the door had just opened and Christiana had stepped out, shepherding their four children toward the path that would lead them to the Shining Gate. Then the gates of the Celestial City closed.

Christian smiled, more content than he could have imagined. The time would come when he would go down to the river to receive the ones he loved. But for now, he would wait with joy for joy. He turned back to the City—someone had put a palm in his hand—and he went, singing, to see the Owner.

I saw only a glimpse of those streets before the gates closed, and I awoke with a start. Behold, it was all a dream.

The sky was the pinkish grey it takes on just before dawn. The air had been washed clear by the night's dew, and the water had beaded on each blade of grass. When the sun came up, sudden and joyous, it shone in brilliant colors from every dewdrop.

I could see the sleepy village far below me. In a short time it would be abustle with chores and business. But for now it seemed still and quiet. Closer was my own house, with a light set in the window, and Jack already yap-yapping at the barn swallows.

I shouldered my pack to make the long journey home.

FAREWELL TO THE READER

Now, reader, I have told my dream to thee;
See if thou canst interpret it to me.
Put by the curtains, look within my veil,
Turn up my sentences, and do not fail.
There, if thou seekest them, such things thou'lt find
As will be helpful to an honest mind.

What of my dross thou findest here? Be bold
To throw away, but yet preserve the Gold.
What if my Gold be wrapped up in ore?
None throws away the apple for the core.
But if thou shalt cast all away as vain,
I know not but 'twill make me dream again.

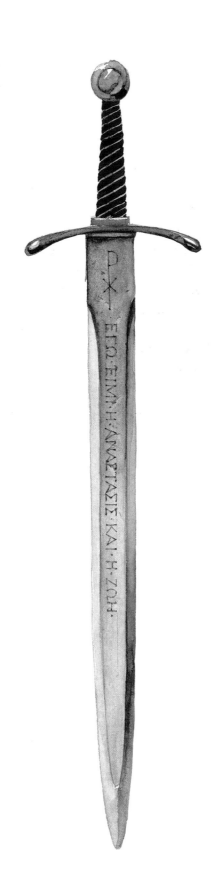

A NOTE ABOUT THIS BOOK

This edition of *Pilgrim's Progress* was designed and illustrated for William B. Eerdmans Publishing Company by Barry Moser. The text was composed in Minion, a typeface designed by Robert Slimbach in 1989 for Adobe Systems. It was based on the Renaissance models of Nicolas Jenson, Francesco Griffo, Claude Garamond, and Robert Granjon. The word *minion*, which means "beloved servant," was used in early typefounding to denote the size of a typeface. The typographer for this book was Donald Prus.

The illustrations were executed in the winter of 1994, in the artist's studio in Hatfield, Massachusetts. They were prepared on paper handmade in 1982 by Simon Green at the Barcham Green Paper Mills located in Maidstone, Kent, Great Britain. The medium is watercolor. It is used in the traditional transparent technique wherein the white of the paper shows through the colors.